THE POCKET PRAYER

by

Pamela Christian Flickinger

Little Rock

2019

Copyright 2020 by Pamela Christian Flickinger

Published by Faith 2 Fe Publishing,
Little Rock AR 72205
www.publishyourfaith.com

ISBN-13: 978-1-949934-25-0

All rights reserved under International Copyright Law. No part of this publication may be reproduced, stored in a retrieval system, or transmitted in any form or by any means-electronic, mechanical, photocopy, recording or any other- except for brief quotations in printed reviews, without the prior written permission of the author.

Unless otherwise noted, all scripture is from the King James Version of the Bible.

Scriptures marked ESV are from the ESV® Bible (The Holy Bible, English Standard Version®), copyright© 2001 by Crossway Bibles, a publishing ministry of Good News Publishers. Used by permission. All rights reserved."

Scriptures marked HCSB are taken from the HOLMAN CHRISTIAN STANDARD BIBLE (HCSB, copyright©1999, 2000, 2002, 2003 by Holman Bible Publishers, Nashville Tennessee. All rights reserved.

Scriptures marked NASB are taken from the New American Standard Bible® (NASB),Copyright © 1960, 1962, 1963, 1968, 1971, 1972, 1973, 1975, 1977, 1995 by The Lockman Foundation Used by permission. www. Lockman.org

Scriptures marked NIV are taken from THE HOLY BIBLE, NEW INTERNATIONAL VERSION ®. Copyright© 1973, 1978, 1984, 2011 by Biblica, Inc.™. Used by permission of Zondervan.

Scriptures marked NLT are taken from the HOLY BIBLE, NEW LIVING TRANSLATION (NLT): Copyright© 1996, 2004, 2007 by Tyndale House Foundation. Used by permission of Tyndale House Publishers, Inc., Carol Stream, Illinois 60188. All rights reserved. Used by permission.

Scripture quotations marked NLV are taken from the New Life Version, copyright © 1969 and 2003. Used by permission of Barbour Publishing, Inc., Uhrichsville, Ohio 44683. All rights reserved.

Scriptures marked NKJV are taken from the NEW KING JAMES VERSION® (NKJV): Copyright© 1982 by Thomas Nelson, Inc. Used by permission. All rights reserved.

Scriptures marked TLB are taken from the THE LIVING BIBLE (TLB): Copyright© 1971. Used by permission of Tyndale House Publishers, Inc.,Carol Stream, Illinois 60188. All rights reserved.

Scriptures marked TLV are taken from the Tree of Life (TLV) Translation of the Bible. Copyright © 2015 by The Messianic Jewish Family Bible Society.

Scripture quotations marked TPT are from The Passion Translation®. Copyright © 2017, 2018 by Passion & Fire Ministries, Inc. Used by permission. All rights reserved. ThePassionTranslation.com.

Dedication

⚜

Your own restriction
is by your own mindset;
Don't allow fear of the unknown
to steal from your destiny

⚜

Matthew 25:14-30
Parable of the Talents
Recognize what's in your hand
...and plant it!

Contents

Dedication	v
Introduction	1
Truth Trumps Fact	5
Our Identity	21
Logos vs. Rhema	37
Addictions	51
Anger, Hatred, Revenge	57
Authority	62
Battles of the Mind	69
Blessing, Favor, Prosperity	76
Children	83
Depression	90
Faith	96
Fear, Anxiety	102
Forgiveness, Offense, Bitterness	110

Guidance, Led by the Spirit	116
Healing	123
Identity, Confidence, Insecurity	130
Joy	137
Love	143
Peace	150
Protection	156
Salvation	164
Strength	171
Wisdom, Understanding	176
Prayer of Salvation	183
About the Author	185
For More Information	186

Introduction

∽

HAVE YOU EVER RECEIVED a word from God about your purpose here on earth, and then, when something is asked of you, you see all the imperfections and reasons why you feel unable to fulfill what He has asked of you?

This book is an example from my life of a word given to me and how I made a list of why I wasn't qualified. I thought, *I have never written a book in my life. I haven't attended Bible college, and I haven't been ordained. So, how could I be qualified to write a book that helps people understand the Word of God and apply it in their life?* That's a lot of pressure!

But with God's never-ending love, I knew that I couldn't put this off any longer. I have received way too many promptings of the Holy Spirit. Many conversations and divine appointments have revealed to me that this is time!

Most people have a vague understanding of the Bible and the stories it tells, but do we truly understand what a powerful tool it is? I was brought up in the Christian faith, learning about Smith Wigglesworth, William Seymour, Maria Woodworth-Etter, John G. Lake, and other generals of God who paved the way before us. Learning about these generals and their stories, I wanted to know how and why God used them so mightily and how they got to be a part of such mighty miracles.

When I read about these miracles and all the wonders God manifested through these people, I asked myself a question, Why not me? If God could work through them, could He could work through me? They knew something about the Bible. I clearly did not. They believed what God said they could do. They believed the Word of God, and if it worked for them, why wouldn't it work for me? I would like to say, "I'm a faith girl," but I was still at a loss to understand how to make the Word work for me.

So, the journey began! I set out to learn about God's Words and the power they hold according to Proverbs 18:21: *The tongue has the power of life and death, and those who love it will eat its*

The Pocket Prayer

fruit (NIV). This is a spiritual law set in the earth that is as real as the law of gravity. I learned to follow the Holy Spirit, His teachings about the Word, the weight the Word carries, the power it holds, the hope it gives, and the faith to carry it out.

Did you know that there are two types of words at work in your life? Words that hold reasoning, using facts and figures, are called *logos* words. The other is a *rhema* word, which refers to a living, active word in your life—like your salvation!

I like to explain it like this. Your salvation is such a great example of a *rhema* word because, no matter what, you can't be talked out of it! You know within your heart (your spirit or your inner man) that you are saved. No one can take that from you! This is a good measuring stick to determine if you have a *rhema* word or *logos* word.

We will be learning about God's Word, and yes, we will gain a lot from *logos*. But what we need are the *rhema* words to take place in our life! This book will help you learn how to take that *logos* word and turn it into a *rhema* word!

Pamela Christian Flickinger

I am very excited to share how the Lord took me on this journey of learning how to apply His Word and see His results! This is a simple truth, yet many don't know how to apply the Word, let alone understand and believe that it is living, active, and can be used today! I pray this book encourages you to take a step of faith, proving to yourself that God's Word works, that it is relevant today, and that you start receiving fruit from it. I know I have, and still receive to this day!

Chapter One

Truth Trumps Fact

AS A MOTHER OF THREE children, there have been many instances where I wanted to fix all of my children's owies, heartbreaks, disappointments, etc. At the age of 27, I was a young mother, expecting my second child, Christian. It was rather a breeze from the pregnancy to the delivery, and we had a healthy baby boy.

But when Christian turned three months old, he became very sick, and we took him to the doctor. The doctor ran tests and came back with the diagnosis of RSV (Respiratory syncytial virus) and severe eczema. As a diligent mom, I administered the breathing treatments as prescribed and applied the topical steroid creams to ease his skin.

During this time, I decided to be thankful that this diagnosis was not something much worse. Within a little over a year, Christian had fewer and fewer breathing treatments. Still, the eczema skin condition was getting worse until the rash and bumps covered his entire body.

The eczema was very itchy and painful to him. I would wake up in the middle of the night to a crying baby who had scratched his skin raw. His pajamas and bedsheets would be soaked in blood. My heart would break, and the tears rolled down my face as I bandaged and treated his raw skin with steroid creams that would add to his pain.

I was a Christian and prayed over my child many times, asking the Lord to heal him. But nothing ever changed. I felt helpless, exhausted, and upset, wondering, *What else could I do to help him?*

One day, I called my sister Rebekah. I was crying and trying to figure out what else could I do! She asked me a question, "Pam, do you know the difference between facts and truth?" I thought she was getting ready to explain some medical terminology since she is also a registered nurse. She explained to me that doctors

The Pocket Prayer

run tests to seek results—the facts about the symptoms. "These are the facts!"

She explained that when we learn these facts about the symptoms, we don't deny that these are the facts about the diagnosis. She went on the tell me that the Word of God is Truth! She declared that the Word of God, the Truth, will trump the facts every time!

So, I had a decision to make. I could choose to stand on the diagnosis of the doctor concerning Christian and deal with all that comes with it, or I could choose to stand on God's Word for my son and believe that His Truth brings healing.

Renewing the Mind

After hearing this new way of thinking, I knew this was a key in getting my son's healing. When we hear something new and try to comprehend it, it takes time to renew our minds and change the way we process our thoughts. I knew if I was going to change my thinking, I needed to find out what the Word, the Truth, says about my situation.

ROMANS 12:2 NIV

2 Do not conform to the pattern of this world, but be transformed by the renewing of your mind. Then you will be able to test and approve what God's will is—his good, pleasing, and perfect will.

***

ROMANS 8: 5-8 NIV

5 Those who live according to the flesh have their minds set on what the flesh desires; but those who live in accordance with the Spirit have their minds set on what the Spirit desires.

6 The mind governed by the flesh is death, but the mind governed by the Spirit is life and peace.

7 The mind governed by the flesh is hostile to God; it does not submit to God's law, nor can it do so.

8 Those who are in the realm of the flesh cannot please God.

***

2 CORINTHIANS 10: 5 NIV

5 We demolish arguments and every pretension that sets itself up against the knowledge of God, and we take captive every thought to make it obedient to Christ.

The Pocket Prayer

There are key points in these scriptures that relate to the importance of our thinking. In Romans 12:2, I love how the Bible says that by the renewing of your mind, you will be able to test and approve what is God's good, pleasing, and perfect will. Yes, please! This will save us so much time and heartache if we know His will for our lives in every area.

In Romans 8:6, the Bible says that a mind governed by the spirit is life and peace. How important this is to know that we have His Word on this! We are not limited to live in fear or worry, but we can live full of life and peace!

Second Corinthians 10:5 powerfully states that the Word of God will demolish anything that tries to be established against it. That is TRUTH trumping the fact! Oh, how I love God's Word! If you can get this TRUTH in your heart, you will become unstoppable!

Not Being Moved

When you start learning how to think right and begin trusting in God's Word,

Pamela Christian Flickinger

be aware that your flesh wants to go back to old ways of handling situations and reasoning, especially when your circumstances grow worse. Don't be surprised or downhearted if you don't see results right away.

There will come a time, in your walk with the Lord, when you have to choose to stand. The enemy wants you to be moved and to think nothing is happening. He wants you to change your confession and compromise your position. Instead, you can stand firm on God's Word and let nothing move you! You will have to come to the point where you believe God's Word is true. It is that simple.

I know when I was standing for my son's healing, the Lord spoke to me, "Pam, if you are not receiving or seeing the results for what you are believing for from Me, the deficiency is never on My end. It is on yours." That was an eye-opener that I needed to hear. I was the one who could "make or break" this situation, but God and His words are life, and truth. They are unmovable! Either I take Him at His Word, or I don't. These are a couple of Scriptures that helped me in this area:

The Pocket Prayer

MARK 11:23-24 NIV

23 "Truly I tell you, if anyone says to this mountain, 'Go, throw yourself into the sea,' and does not doubt in their heart but believes that what they say will happen, it will be done for them.

24 Therefore I tell you, whatever you ask for in prayer, believe that you have received it, and it will be yours.

I love this Scripture because it identifies that the responsibility to believe is all on us. YOU CAN'T DOUBT! YOU CAN'T BE MOVED! You must BELIEVE what the Truth says is the final authority—period!

Another Scripture that helped me settle this debate in my mind is:

JAMES 1: 5-8, 22-25 NIV

5 If any of you lacks wisdom, you should ask God, who gives generously to all without finding fault, and it will be given to you.

6 But when you ask, you must believe and not doubt, because the one who doubts is like a wave of the sea, blown and tossed by the wind.

7 That person should not expect to receive anything from the Lord.

Pamela Christian Flickinger

8 Such a person is double-minded and unstable in all they do.

***

22 Do not merely listen to the word, and so deceive yourselves. Do what it says.

23 Anyone who listens to the word but does not do what it says is like someone who looks at his face in a mirror

24 and, after looking at himself, goes away and immediately forgets what he looks like.

25 But whoever looks intently into the perfect law that gives freedom, and continues in it—not forgetting what they have heard, but doing it—they will be blessed in what they do.

I love this chapter in James! The Scripture plainly says in verse 6 that you must believe and not doubt. The person who allows doubt to enter is like waves of the sea. The emotions of a wavering person allow them to be moved and to be tossed back and forth in their thinking. Verse 7 reveals that this person shouldn't expect to receive anything from the Lord because they are double-minded in all they do.

The Pocket Prayer

I know this Scripture doesn't paint a flowery picture with rainbows and butterflies. It may seem quite harsh. But if you want this to work for you, you have to choose to believe God is telling you the Truth. You must believe His Word is something on which you can stand firm. Otherwise, you will see Him as a God that doesn't keep His Word and doesn't really mean what He says.

The Word is Final Authority

In James 1:25, the Bible explains that we have to make that choice, allowing God's Word to become the final authority in our lives, allowing it to trump every fact that we encounter. This process doesn't happen overnight. It takes time to get our mind and heart wrapped around this Truth!

In these next Scriptures, we see that God's Word will outlast my life, my children's life, and so forth. His Word does not stop working. It as an ever-continuing move of the Spirit that will perform what it was set out to do. To understand that you can speak the Word over your children, grandchildren, and great-grandchildren, and they will walk in blessings and wisdom because of your willingness to get a hold of these truths is something to get excited about!

Let's take time to read and meditate on these verses:

ISAIAH 55:11 NIV

11 so is my word that goes out from my mouth: It will not return to me empty, but will accomplish what I desire and achieve the purpose for which I sent it.

* * *

ISAIAH 40:8 NIV

8 The grass withers and the flowers fall, but the word of our God endures forever.

* * *

MATTHEW 24:35 NIV

35 Heaven and earth will pass away, but my words will never pass away.

After receiving these Scriptures and getting them down in your spirit, you might dare to read Luke 10:19 and believe what it says! Yes, you guessed

The Pocket Prayer

it! Luke 10:19 is another one of my favorites! When the Word becomes your final authority, you will realize how much God wants you to walk in victory and all the blessings in this life. But we need to understand that we have a crucial part to play in this. WE MUST BELIEVE!

Four Types of Soil

In Mark 4:1-20, we read the parable of the sower.

MARK 4:1-20 (NIV)

1 Again Jesus began to teach by the lake. The crowd that gathered around him was so large that he got into a boat and sat in it out on the lake, while all the people were along the shore at the water's edge.

2 He taught them many things by parables, and in his teaching said:

3 "Listen! A farmer went out to sow his seed.

4 As he was scattering the seed, some fell along the path, and the birds came and ate it up.

5 Some fell on rocky places, where it did not have much soil. It sprang up quickly, because the soil was shallow.

Pamela Christian Flickinger

6 But when the sun came up, the plants were scorched, and they withered because they had no root.

7 Other seed fell among thorns, which grew up and choked the plants, so that they did not bear grain.

8 Still other seed fell on good soil. It came up, grew and produced a crop, some multiplying thirty, some sixty, some a hundred times."

9 Then Jesus said, "Whoever has ears to hear, let them hear."

10 When he was alone, the Twelve and the others around him asked him about the parables.

11 He told them, "The secret of the kingdom of God has been given to you. But to those on the outside everything is said in parables

12 so that, they may be ever seeing but never perceiving, and ever hearing but never understanding; otherwise they might turn and be forgiven!

13 Then Jesus said to them, "Don't you understand this parable? How then will you understand any parable?

14 The farmer sows the word.

15 Some people are like seed along the path,

The Pocket Prayer

where the word is sown. As soon as they hear it, Satan comes and takes away the word that was sown in them.

16 Others, like seed sown on rocky places, hear the word and at once receive it with joy.

17 But since they have no root, they last only a short time. When trouble or persecution comes because of the word, they quickly fall away.

18 Still others, like seed sown among thorns, hear the word;

19 but the worries of this life, the deceitfulness of wealth and the desires for other things come in and choke the word, making it unfruitful.

20 Others, like seed sown on good soil, hear the word, accept it, and produce a crop—some thirty, some sixty, some a hundred times what was sown."

There are so many "nuggets" in Mark 4 that we need to grasp as we learn about God's Word and how to apply it in our lives. Jesus really emphasizes how important it is to be good ground so that when the Word is sown (planted) in our life, we do our part to produce fruit from it!

It's very important that we pay attention to the very first type of ground.

Far too often, we hear a good word that really ministers to us and sparks something inside of us. We truly want to get a hold of what the Lord is trying to get across. But be aware! Those are the words that Satan does not want you to have!

I don't know how many times this has happened to me. The enemy swoops in, with distractions, chaos, business, or you name it. He can use it to distract you and steal that word out from right under your nose. Be aware of his devices in this area of your life. Know your weaknesses because he more than likely knows them better than you do. Stand firm, and don't let go of those words that God is waiting on you to receive.

Read this passage of Scripture slowly and recognize the importance of God's Word. Don't compromise your position by letting it go. Don't be talked out of what's rightfully yours!

In verse 11, Jesus tells us something very powerful:

MARK 4:11 NIV

11 He told them, "The secret of the kingdom of

The Pocket Prayer

God has been given to you. But to those on the outside everything is said in parables.

Then, He goes on to say in verse 12, why the Lord caused it to be this way. With our heart's as the soil, we hear the Word, accept it, believe it, tend to it, cultivate it, and we produce a crop/fruit from it. The Word becomes active in our lives.

The extent that you tend to the Word, meditating on it, will depend on you. It will determine how much of a crop you'll produce from it, some thirty, sixty, and some a hundred times. That is the goal of this book—for you to see that His Word works and know that you can actually use it in your life now!

Chapter Two

Our Identity

HAVE YOU EVER FELT LIKE a puzzle piece that didn't quite fit? I have dealt with this my entire life. Many people have said, "Pam, you are unique." I've heard this so much as I've grown up. I heard it at church and at home. I thought it was people's way of telling me to try harder to blend in and to stop being so different.

After many years of never seeming to "fit in," I realized that I was made to NOT "fit in." I was created to be different. The Lord says in His Word that we are a peculiar people, a holy nation, a royal priesthood, His own special people (1 Peter 2:9 NIV).

In Jeremiah 1:5 (NIV), the Lord says, *"Before I formed you in the womb I knew you,, before you were born I set you apart."*

God knew me and chose me! He made me and created me to have what I think are weaknesses. But those weaknesses are where my power lies in Him. Paul knew this.

2 CORINTHIANS 12:9 NIV

9 But he said to me, "My grace is sufficient for you, for my power is made perfect in weakness." Therefore I will boast all the more gladly about my weaknesses, so that Christ's power may rest on me.

It is so powerful to know that the God Who made everything you see around you, He chose you, set you apart, created your likes and dislikes, what gives you hope, what gives you drive, and what makes you angry. (See Jer. 29:11.)

The Lord meticulously formed your DNA, your fingerprints, and your retinas to make only one YOU! Since He put that much thought and effort into making you, it proves you are not a mistake! You are not here by accident. You are predestined to be here with all of your unique qualities, placed in this time, in this day, to fulfill what only you were sent here to do with the deposits that are inside of you!

See, we try so hard to be like everyone else, but our Father in Heaven only wants us to be who He created us to be.

The Pocket Prayer

PSALM 139:14-17 NIV

14 I praise you because I am fearfully and wonderfully made; your works are wonderful, I know that full well.

15 My frame was not hidden from you when I was made in the secret place, when I was woven together in the depths of the earth.

16 Your eyes saw my unformed body; all the days ordained for me were written in your book before one of them came to be.

17 How precious to me are your thoughts, God! How vast is the sum of them!

We need to be aware of our own individuality and learn our strengths (although they may look like weaknesses to us). We should learn what "lights us up" and what triggers us to doubt and be angry. You may wonder why I am telling you to learn this. It is because God will relate to each of us differently according to how He made us.

Scripture Can Relate to us Differently

When you are reading the Word or

spending time in prayer, how do you hear or know when God is talking to you? Some read books or the Bible, and the words will jump off the page at them. While others hear a still small voice inside of them. Some people have dreams and visions, hear an audible voice, or sense His presence right there in the room.

God has many ways to get our attention. We just need to understand that He's going to relate to us in line with how He made us.

EPHESIANS 4:7 NLT

7 However, he has given each one of us a special gift through the generosity of Christ.

When you are reading a passage of the Scripture, it may seem like you are just reading another line of a book. But someone else can read that very same Scripture and its full of life, hope, direction, and insight to them. We can't compare our gifts and callings to each other because we all have a part to play and contribute.

ROMANS 12:4-8 NIV

4 For just as each of us has one body with many

The Pocket Prayer

members, and these members do not all have the same function,

5 so in Christ we, though many, form one body, and each member belongs to all the others.

6 We have different gifts, according to the grace given to each of us. If your gift is prophesying, then prophesy in accordance with your faith;

7 if it is serving, then serve; if it is teaching, then teach;

8 if it is to encourage, then give encouragement; if it is giving, then give generously; if it is to lead, do it diligently; if it is to show mercy, do it cheerfully.

We each have an assignment to fulfill in the Body of Christ, and we aren't all called to do the same thing. We are all different, set apart, and gifted differently for a purpose.

EPHESIANS 4:11-13 NLT

11 Now these are the gifts Christ gave to the church: the apostles, the prophets, the evangelists, and the pastors and teachers.

12 Their responsibility is to equip God's people to do his work and build up the church, the body of Christ.

13 This will continue until we all come to such

unity in our faith and knowledge of God's Son that we will be mature in the Lord, measuring up to the full and complete standard of Christ.

When we start understanding ourselves, recognizing our giftings, and how God made us unique, then it becomes easier for us to understand others and the "hows and whys" of their unique operations as well.

1 PETER 4:10 NLT

10 God has given each of you a gift from his great variety of spiritual gifts. Use them well to serve one another.

* * *

PROVERBS 18:21

21 Death and life are in the power of the tongue: and they that love it shall eat the fruit thereof.

When learning that you are unique, created for a purpose, and predestined for such a time as now, you will begin to understand more about your true identity.

One summer afternoon, I was at my kitchen sink, washing baby bottles. I was exhausted. The Lord spoke to me audibly with such clarity, love, and in a distinct straightforward tone, and said,

The Pocket Prayer

"Don't you know that you're a daughter of the Most High?!" I stood there with all my motherly duties staring back at me, feeling lost in the midst of exhaustion and clutter, almost in disbelief of what I just heard. I can truly say that my life changed after this encounter.

The Holy Spirit took me on a journey of learning my true identity as a daughter of the King! He had me research what a kingdom is like and how it is governed. Since I live in a democracy where we have rights as citizens, are allowed to vote, and have a say about things, the Lord needed me to understand the difference. He needed me to see from where I come, to whom I belong, and what that means for me here and now.

There are some foundational pieces in the Word that I want to establish before we go any further. In the beginning, God created the heavens and the earth. He spoke them into existence. (Gen. 1:1) But as you go further into Genesis, notice what God said in verse 3: *"And God said, Let there be light."*

This pattern continues:
- in verse 6, *"And God said...,"*

- in verse 9, *"And God said...,"*
- in verse 11, *"Then God said...,"*
- in verse 14, *"And God said...,"*

Next, let's read verses 26-28:

GENESIS 1:26-28 NIV

26 Then God said, "Let us make mankind in our image, in our likeness, so that they may rule over the fish in the sea and the birds in the sky, over the livestock and all the wild animals, and over all the creatures that move along the ground."

27 So God created mankind in his own image, in the image of God he created them; male and female he created them.

28 God blessed them and said to them, "Be fruitful and increase in number; fill the earth and subdue it. Rule over the fish in the sea and the birds in the sky and over every living creature that moves on the ground."

This is so very important for us to understand because it explains how God wanted the earth to work. The Lord delegated the authority to man, to govern and rule the earth. This was established from the beginning.

So, you may ask, "How is that supposed to pertain to us today?" We know Adam and Eve fell from their

The Pocket Prayer

position when they disobeyed God's Word. In their disobedience, they gave their authority over to Satan (Gen. 3).

When Jesus came to the earth (He is referred to as the last Adam in 1 Cor. 15:45), He died for us. Jesus went to hell for us, so we never have to go. He took the keys of death, defeated Satan, and rose from the grave, making a show of His victory openly (Col. 2:15). Jesus returned the authority to rule and reign here on earth to mankind!

MARK 16:15-20 NIV

15 He said to them, "Go into all the world and preach the gospel to all creation.

16 Whoever believes and is baptized will be saved, but whoever does not believe will be condemned.

17 And these signs will accompany those who believe: In my name they will drive out demons; they will speak in new tongues;

18 they will pick up snakes with their hands; and when they drink deadly poison, it will not hurt them at all; they will place their hands on sick people, and they will get well."

19 After the Lord Jesus had spoken to them,

he was taken up into heaven and he sat at the right hand of God.

20 Then the disciples went out and preached everywhere, and the Lord worked with them and confirmed his word by the signs that accompanied it.

Since Jesus set everything right again, the way that God intended it to be in the beginning, it's important to understand that the earth is ours. We are heirs of God. We need to take our place and understand our role in the earth.

When the Lord told me that I was a daughter of the Most High, I had to discover what that entailed. He showed me these Scriptures that defined what a daughter or son of God looked and acted like.

There is one Scripture in particular that I want to share with you. One of the reasons behind the writing of this book is for you to understand that there is power within your words. God made mankind to rule and subdue the earth. When a king makes a decree or a decision either for his country or his people, the decree is carried out, with no questions asked. They are to be done, period!

The Pocket Prayer

In Genesis, we see that God spoke things into existence, *"And God said..."* Then, God said, *"Let's make man in our own image and likeness."* We are His sons and daughters with the ability to decree and declare things on purpose here on the earth.

The Lord gave me this Scripture that shows this spiritual law that He put into place from the beginning when He spoke:

PROVERBS 18:21 NIV

21 The tongue has the power of life and death, and those who love it will eat its fruit.

The things we speak release life or death. This spiritual law is as real as the law of gravity. You don't have to believe in gravity to experience the reality of it. In the same way, whether you are a believer or nonbeliever, your words have the power to release life or death. You will eat the fruit of whatever you are speaking.

I looked into the Word of God to see this truth at work.

MATTHEW 21:18-22 NIV

18 Early in the morning, as Jesus was on his way back to the city, he was hungry.

Pamela Christian Flickinger

19 Seeing a fig tree by the road, he went up to it but found nothing on it except leaves. Then he said to it, "May you never bear fruit again!" Immediately the tree withered.

20 When the disciples saw this, they were amazed. "How did the fig tree wither so quickly?" they asked.

21 Jesus replied, "Truly I tell you, if you have faith and do not doubt, not only can you do what was done to the fig tree, but also you can say to this mountain, 'Go, throw yourself into the sea,' and it will be done.

22 If you believe, you will receive whatever you ask for in prayer."

* * *

LUKE 4:38-39 NIV

38 Jesus left the synagogue and went to the home of Simon. Now Simon's mother-in-law was suffering from a high fever, and they asked Jesus to help her.

39 So he bent over her and rebuked the fever, and it left her. She got up at once and began to wait on them.

NOTE: Jesus didn't pray over Simon Peter's mother-n-law. Instead, Jesus spoke to the fever!

The Pocket Prayer

MATTHEW 8:16

16 When evening came, many who were demon-possessed were brought to him, and he drove out the spirits with a word and healed all the sick.

Jesus knew His authority, and He knew that a spoken word would set His authority into motion. That sounds like a kingdom mindset. There are so many examples of this throughout the Word of God. The centurion understood authority and acknowledged that by Jesus speaking the word, his servant would be healed (Matt. 8:5-13). In another example, Jesus spoke to His disciples about "going to the other side." When a storm came up during their journey, Jesus spoke to the storm to calm it.

LUKE 8:22-25 NIV

22 One day Jesus said to his disciples, "Let us go over to the other side of the lake." So they got into a boat and set out.

23 As they sailed, he fell asleep. A squall came down on the lake, so that the boat was being swamped, and they were in great danger.

24 The disciples went and woke him, saying, "Master, Master, we're going to drown! "He

got up and rebuked the wind and the raging waters; the storm subsided, and all was calm.

25 "Where is your faith?" he asked his disciples. In fear and amazement they asked one another, "Who is this? He commands even the winds and the water, and they obey him."

Jesus knew He was going to the other side. He spoke it! But the disciples didn't believe that word. They woke Him up, and Jesus spoke to the storm and calmed it. He asked them, "Where is your faith?" But they let doubt and unbelief steal that word from them.

I choose to believe God's Word is true, and it is life! Some would say, "Well, that's Jesus and the disciples who did all those things." I would say that there are many accounts that occurred long afterward where miracles have happened, and the Word has gone forth. The ones who knew this truth also knew who they were and their purpose. They have accomplished the greater things which Jesus spoke of in John 14:12.

JOHN 14:12-14 NIV

12 Very truly I tell you, whoever believes in me will do the works I have been doing, and they

The Pocket Prayer

will do even greater things than these, because I am going to the Father.

13 And I will do whatever you ask in my name, so that the Father may be glorified in the Son.

14 You may ask me for anything in my name, and I will do it.

Some of my most treasured stories are the ones about the great generals of faith who have come before us. Those men and women are proof that the Word works, and God is no respecter of persons, but He responds to those who have faith in His Word! I can't go into the details of every story of the generals of faith to list all of the mighty things God was able to do through them, but there are a few that I would love to share with you.

Smith Wigglesworth had many miracles in his ministry, including having more than one person raised from the dead. William Branham had amazing testimonies of God working through him, but some of my favorites are of those who were blind receiving their sight.

There were the Healing Homes of John G. Lake and the revivals in the late 1800s with Maria Woodworth-Etter.

Pamela Christian Flickinger

I love hearing and reading books about the great revival in the early 1900s that took place on Azusa Street in California, and how God used William Seymour as he prayed with his head in a box. The list goes on and on of the people who dared to believe that the Word of God is true and walked in the power of His Word while here on earth. If you haven't read about some of these generals of faith, I encourage you to do so. It will build up your faith!

Jesus did say that even greater things shall even we do, and, yes, I know that great things are yet to come for you!

Chapter Three

Logos vs. Rhema

I WANT TO LOOK MORE closely at these two words: *logos* and *rhema*. It is important for you to understand the difference in them to comprehend how *The Pocket Prayer* will work in your life.

A *logos* word is objectively recorded in the Bible. We understand Jesus is the living Logos recorded in John 1:1. Jesus became the Living Word of God here on earth. In Hebrews 4:12, we learn the *logos* of God (the Bible) is living and active, sharper than any two-edged sword.

Then, in First Corinthians 2: 12-13, we, as children of God, receive *logos* through the Holy Spirit. He teaches truth, brings understanding, and gives wisdom. Isn't it amazing? In this interaction with the Holy Spirit, God has given us so much!

Many of us love to read the Word of God and books that teach us and help us grow up spiritually. But if we don't do anything with the Word, we just gain knowledge of the Word.

One way I could describe a *rhema* word from God is to say it is one of the greatest gifts you could ever receive! A *rhema* word is like receiving a download from God or having the Spirit of God directly visit with you for a specific reason.

You may be thinking, WOW! That sounds truly amazing. I can tell you, the most amazing events that have happened in my life are *rhema* moments. *Rhema* words are more than just the knowledge of the Word. They are living and active among us. There were many instances in the Bible when the *rhema* of God showed up, and when it did, people were completely changed by it.

For instance, Jesus spoke to the woman at the well and told her about everything she had done in her life (John 4). Another example occurred with the woman who suffered the issue of blood (Mark 5:25-34). She had faith that with just a touch, she would be healed, and she received her *rhema* word.

But in that story, there were many

The Pocket Prayer

people touching Jesus, and nothing happened for them. They may have heard and learned about what Jesus had done. They had an understanding of him as *logos*. But the woman with the issue of blood had a *rhema* word. It was living and active inside of her, so much so that Jesus felt the power when it went out from Him! That's how you know when the Word works—power is accessed!

There are times I have tried to explain the difference between *logos* and *rhema* to people who aren't sure if they have ever had a *rhema* word before. I ask them if they have been saved. Have they asked Jesus into their hearts and lives? The answer is, usually, "Yes."

Then, I ask them, "After you were saved, did you receive a certificate from heaven, stating that you have been saved?" I usually get strange looks at this point and go on to ask them if they've been to heaven to see the Lamb's Book of Life to verify that their name is written in there.

They respond, "Well, no."

So, I proceed to ask them, "How do you know that you are saved?"

They tell me that they know in here while pointing at their heart. I ask them if I could talk them out of their salvation, and they assure me, "Absolutely not!"

I explain that their salvation is real and active, living on the inside of them. It is not just head knowledge. It is a *rhema* word to them.

This is what I like to use as my measuring stick of belief. If you can be talked out of it or convinced otherwise, it hasn't become a *rhema* word in your life yet. But if you choose to grab hold of a word, like the woman with the issue of blood, no one will stop you, take it from you, or make you change your mind. It becomes as steadfast as your salvation, and it is yours! So, an easy way to check yourself is to use your measuring stick of salvation. This will give you a clear understanding if you have a *rhema* or if you are still working on it.

The Lord started showing me that His Word is the final authority, and that we just need to believe it to the point that it becomes rhema in our life so nothing could take it away from us. I had suffered from kidney and bladder infections close

The Pocket Prayer

to 13 years. I had them so often that I became allergic to a long list of antibiotics having to take them so much during this time. I knew the Word of God said that healing was mine (*logos*). I didn't quite know how to receive the *rhema* of that word.

One day, the Holy Spirit led me over to Romans, the 8th chapter.

ROMANS 8:1-2 NIV

1 Therefore, there is now no condemnation for those who are in Christ Jesus,

2 because through Christ Jesus the law of the Spirit who gives life has set you free from the law of sin and death.

As I read this text, I saw a vision play out in my mind. I was in a courtroom, standing up at the defendant's table with Jesus standing beside me. I looked across to see who was standing at the prosecutor's table, and it was Satan. He wasn't in the stereotypical, red-horned outfit.

Instead, he was dressed to the nines in the finest of suits, and he reeked of arrogance. He had a huge stack of papers in front of him, seemingly boastful about the case he undoubtedly felt he was about to win.

I looked to the front of the courtroom, and a great man entered the room. God Almighty was presiding over the rulings. He was in a judge's robe, and when He walked, it was with such authority that my chest felt as it would burst from the pounding of thunder in His every step. I noticed that He had a beautiful white shining beard, and His whole face shone with glory.

I knew that I was the one on trial. Satan, the accuser of the brethren, had plenty of accusations to use against me, having kept account of all the wrongs I had done. Satan boastfully stated a case against me, hurling accusations, sickness, bitterness, anything he could find to use against me.

Then, Jesus stood. With a calm, steadfastness in His voice, He told the Judge, God, the Father, that in the law of spirit of life, it clearly states that through Him, I am free from the law of sin and death.

Satan stood there, frantically searching to find more accusations to

The Pocket Prayer

use against me. Jesus looked at him and said, "My law, the law of the spirit of life, overrules your law of sin and death."

The vision was over, and I was aware of my surroundings again. I saw this verse in a completely new light. It came alive in me! It was my *rhema* word that I had been waiting for!

So, Romans 8:1-2 became a great pocket prayer for me! I had such a clear perception that anything that falls under the category of sin and death has been overruled by the law of the spirit of life. I knew this truth belonged to me! The years I had struggled with infections were times that the law of sin and death was dominating. But I have a greater law to abide in—the law of the spirit of life. Glory to God!

I wrote this Scripture on a piece of paper and kept it in my pocket. Everywhere I went, I carried this with me. I could read this Scripture over and over, receiving this *logos*, which had become a *rhema* word. When symptoms would show up in my body, I took my *Pocket Prayer* out to renew my mind with what the Word had to say about it. I would stand and not waver from that Word.

It is possible that I read it a thousand times. I was relentless, knowing that this was for me, that healing was mine! Symptoms would show up out of nowhere, trying to talk me out of what was rightfully mine, not just once but constantly.

Satan doesn't like to lose ground, and he especially doesn't want us to gain this kind of power over him and be able to enforce it. That is why it's important to use the Word. God's Word contains the law of the spirit of life!

Why do I put the Scripture in my pocket? Well, one reason is that the Holy Spirit told me to do it. He told me to keep the Word ever before my eyes, not just in my memory (Josh. 1:8). Satan can talk you out of something that you have said or memorized. He is so cunning that he changed Eve's perception of the Word of God and deceived her.

Think about that! Eve knew God. She walked with Him, communed with Him, and should have known better. Yet

Satan used the Word and manipulated it to deceive her.

A couple of months after the vision of the courtroom, I was still standing and believing with Hebrews 8:1-2 as my *Pocket Prayer*. I came down with another kidney infection that was so severe. There was blood in my urine, and my back was in so much pain that I could barely stand upright.

I made a doctor's appointment, and he told me that since I am allergic to everything, he would have to run tests. He explained it would take up to 48 hours to get it back. I sunk down in my chair in pain. I left the doctor's office in defeat, knowing I would have to wait two more days in pain.

In the parking lot, I stood by my car, beyond frustrated, thinking, *I have to deal with this for two more days!* Then, I stopped myself in the middle of my pity party and said, "There is NO WAY am I doing that!"

I pulled my *Pocket Prayer* out and said out loud in the parking lot, "Infection, you are under the law of sin and death. Jesus' law of the spirit of life has set me free from you! So, Lord, I thank You that I am healed according to Your law!"

Then, standing there in faith, believing that His Word trumps my facts, I was done playing around and dealing with this sickness. In just thirty seconds, every pain down my back subsided, and I could stand up straight! I kept thanking the Lord for my healing and went on back home, praising Him the whole way!

Two days later, my doctor called me to tell me the results and express his concern that the infection could have possibly entered my bloodstream by now. He asked me to come straight into the ER.

Instead, I told him that the Lord healed me that day in the parking lot after I left his office. I assured him that I had not experienced any more issues or symptoms since that day. He asked me again if I was sure that I was well. "Yes," I told him, "I am so excited that the Lord healed me!"

So, it is your turn to take that circumstance or situation and see God work in your life. You might wonder, "Okay. How do I get started?" It is easy! The remainder of this book is filled with

The Pocket Prayer

subjects that can be conquered by the Word of God. Find the Scripture that speaks to you specifically.

Do you remember that I stated earlier in the book that we aren't all alike, that you need a Scripture that relates to you? You will know when you find it. There will be a knowing on the inside of you.

Please understand what I mean by this statement: It is NOT about quantity, but it is about quality! So many believers think if they read enough Word, listen to enough teaching, or hear enough praise and worship that it will be more than enough to gain their victory. But it is hard enough with time and focus to gain one *rhema* word, let alone multiple Scriptures at the same time.

All you need is one Word on which to stand, and you will receive your Rhema! There have been many other circumstances and situations in my life in which I have received victories by using different Pocket Prayers.

It's time for you to find your Scripture, write it down, and keep it on you at all times like a soldier keeps his weapons ready at all times. Satan will want to steal this from you. But, remember, God's Word is Truth, and it trumps any facts that Satan can find.

It sounds like a "David-and-Goliath" situation. But David knew who his God was, and he knew that God couldn't be defeated! Satan has no problem making his "Goliath" appear huge, loud, and scary in your life. He is trying to make you doubt and waiver.

David didn't fit into the mold of a soldier. Instead, he was a boy who knew what his God was capable of doing, David knew he didn't have to have the sword or armor of a soldier, that he wasn't fashioned like the others. He was unique, different. He stood against Goliath with just a slingshot, some stones, and the backing of his God. So, it's your turn to take your slingshot and stones (your *rhema* word and your *Pocket Prayer*) and receive your victory!

One Final Encouragement

I want to remind you what the Word says about doubt and wavering

The Pocket Prayer

JAMES 1:2-8 NIV

2 Consider it pure joy, my brothers and sisters, whenever you face trials of many kinds,

3 because you know that the testing of your faith produces perseverance.

4 Let perseverance finish its work so that you may be mature and complete, not lacking anything.

5 If any of you lacks wisdom, you should ask God, who gives generously to all without finding fault, and it will be given to you.

6 But when you ask, you must believe and not doubt, because the one who doubts is like a wave of the sea, blown and tossed by the wind.

7 That person should not expect to receive anything from the Lord.

8 Such a person is double-minded and unstable in all they do.

The Bible says you must believe and not doubt because the one who doubts is double-minded, unstable in all he does. Make sure your words line up with your confession (Pro. 18:21). This may be difficult to accept, but the Word works. If it is not working, it's not because the

Lord changed His mind. It is because we are short-circuiting something on our end.

Stand firm and know that the Lord is helping us all to become mature in these things, not lacking anything (Jas. 1:4)! That should encourage you immensely, knowing that God does not want us to lack anything He has for us!

I am so excited for you to take this step of faith and use God's Word for your life. For some, this may sound too simple to work. Again, I like to compare it to how you received your salvation. You said a prayer, believed it was true, gained eternal life, and became a son/daughter of the Most High. You gained citizenship in heaven! Was that hard? Yet you gained so much!

We are the ones that make it difficult. The Lord has made it very easy. Your salvation is such a great measuring stick through this process. I know God is no respecter of persons, and if He has done this time and time again for me, why wouldn't He do it for you?!

Now, it is time for you to stand and believe!

Addictions

༄

1 JOHN 1:8 (NKJV) If we say that we have no sin, we deceive ourselves, and the truth is not in us.

GALATIANS 5:24 (NLT) Those who belong to Christ Jesus have nailed the passions and desires of their sinful nature to his cross and crucified them there.

HEBREWS 10:23 (HCSB) Let us hold on to the confession of our hope without wavering, for He who promised is faithful.

PSALM 51:2 (HCSB) Wash away my guilt and cleanse me from my sin.

PSALM 79:9 (TPT) Our hero, come and rescue us! O God of the breakthrough, for the glory of your name, come and help us! Forgive and restore us; heal us and cover us in your love.

ROMANS 13:14 (NIV) Rather, clothe yourselves with the Lord Jesus Christ,

Pamela Christian Flickinger

and do not think about how to gratify the desires of the flesh.

ROMANS 6:18 (HCSB) and having been liberated from sin, you became enslaved to righteousness.

ROMANS 6:6 (HCSB) For we know that our old self was crucified with Him in order that sin's dominion over the body may be abolished, so that we may no longer be enslaved to sin,

GALATIANS 5:1(NIV) It is for freedom that Christ has set us free. Stand firm, then, and do not let yourselves be burdened again by a yoke of slavery.

COLOSSIANS 3:5 (ESV) Put to death therefore what is earthly in you: sexual immorality, impurity, passion, evil desire, and covetousness, which is idolatry.

PROVERBS 20:1 (NIV) Wine is a mocker and beer a brawler; whoever is led astray by them is not wise.

ROMANS 12:1 (ESV) I appeal to you therefore, brothers, by the mercies of God, to present your bodies as a living sacrifice, holy and acceptable to God, which is your spiritual worship.

2 CORINTHIANS 5:17 (NLT) This means that anyone who belongs to Christ has become a new person. The old life is gone; a new life has begun!

ROMANS 6:16 (NLT) Don't you realize that you become the slave of whatever you choose to obey? You can be a slave to sin, which leads to death, or you can choose to obey God, which leads to righteous living.

1 CORINTHIANS 15:33 (TPT) So stop fooling yourselves! Evil companions will corrupt good morals and character.

1 JOHN 2:16 (NASB) For all that is in the world, the lust of the flesh and the lust of the eyes and the boastful pride of life, is not from the Father, but is from the world.

1 CORINTHIANS 10:13 (NIV) No temptation has overtaken you except what is common to mankind. And God is faithful; he will not let you be tempted beyond what you can bear. But when you

are tempted, he will also provide a way out so that you can endure it.

1 CORINTHIANS 8:9 (NKJV) But beware lest somehow this liberty of yours become a stumbling block to those who are weak.

EPHESIANS 5:8 (NLT) For once you were full of darkness, but now you have light from the Lord. So live as people of light!

1 CORINTHIANS 5:11 (NIV) But now I am writing to you that you must not associate with anyone who claims to be a brother or sister but is sexually immoral or greedy, an idolater or slanderer, a drunkard or swindler. Do not even eat with such people.

EPHESIANS 5:17-18 (TPT)
17 And don't live foolishly for then you will have discernment to fully understand God's will.

18 And don't get drunk with wine, which is rebellion; instead be filled with the fullness of the Holy Spirit.

The Pocket Prayer

ROMANS 8:37 (TPT) Yet even in the midst of all these things, we triumph over them all, for God has made us to be more than conquerors, and his demonstrated love is our glorious victory over everything!

JOHN 10:10 (NKJV) The thief does not come except to steal, and to kill, and to destroy. I have come that they may have life, and that they may have it more abundantly.

JOHN 8:36 (TPT) So if the Son sets you free from sin, then become a true son and be unquestionably free!

COLOSSIANS 1:13-14 (HCSB)
13 He has rescued us from the domain of darkness and transferred us into the kingdom of the Son He loves.

14 We have redemption, the forgiveness of sins, in Him.

EPHESIANS 4:22-24 (MSG) But that's no life for you. You learned Christ! My assumption is that you have paid careful attention to him, been well instructed in the truth precisely as we have it in Jesus.

Since, then, we do not have the excuse of ignorance, everything—and I do mean everything—connected with that old way of life has to go. It's rotten through and through. Get rid of it! And then take on an entirely new way of life—a God-fashioned life, a life renewed from the inside and working itself into your conduct as God accurately reproduces his character in you.

PHILIPPIANS 4:13 (HCSB) I am able to do all things through Him who strengthens me.

JOHN 8:32 (NLT) And you will know the truth, and the truth will set you free.

Anger, Hatred, Revenge

∽

PROVERBS 19:11 (NLT) Sensible people control their temper; they earn respect by overlooking wrongs.

PROVERBS 15:18 (NLT) A hot-tempered person starts fights; a cool-tempered person stops them.

PROVERBS 15:1 (NKJV) A soft answer turns away wrath, But a harsh word stirs up anger.

PROVERBS 22:24-25 (NIV)
24 Do not make friends with a hot-tempered person, do not associate with one easily angered,

25 or you may learn their ways and get yourself ensnared.

PROVERBS 25:28 (NLT) A person without self-control is like a city with broken-down walls.

PSALM 30:5 (NLT) For his anger lasts only a moment but his favor lasts a lifetime! Weeping may last through the night, but joy comes with the morning.

PSALM 37:8 (ESV) Refrain from anger, and forsake wrath! Fret not yourself; it tends only to evil.

PSALM 145:8 (NIV) The LORD is gracious and compassionate, slow to anger and rich in love.

ISAIAH 54:17 (ESV) no weapon that is fashioned against you shall succeed, and you shall refute every tongue that rises against you in judgment. This is the heritage of the servants of the LORD and their vindication from me, declares the LORD.

COLOSSIANS 3:8 (NKJV) But now you yourselves are to put off all these: anger, wrath, malice, blasphemy, filthy language out of your mouth.

COLOSSIANS 3:21 (NLT) Fathers, do not aggravate your children, or they will become discouraged.

ECCLESIASTES 7:9 (NLT) Control your temper, for anger labels you a fool.

EPHESIANS 4:26 (ESV) Be angry and do not sin; do not let the sun go down on your anger,

EPHESIANS 4:31-32 (NIV)
31 Get rid of all bitterness, rage and anger, brawling and slander, along with every form of malice.

32 Be kind and compassionate to one another, forgiving each other, just as in Christ God forgave you.

HEBREWS 10:30 (NKJV) For we know Him who said, "Vengeance is Mine, I will repay," says the Lord. And again, "The LORD will judge His people."

HEBREWS 2:18 (NLT) Since he himself has gone through suffering and testing, he is able to help us when we are being tested.

2 PETER 1:5-8 (NIV)
5 For this very reason, make every effort to add to your faith goodness; and to goodness, knowledge;
6 and to knowledge, self-control; and to self-control, perseverance; and to perseverance, godliness;

7 and to godliness, mutual affection; and to mutual affection, love.

8 For if you possess these qualities in increasing measure, they will keep you from being ineffective and unproductive in your knowledge of our Lord Jesus Christ.

JAMES 1:19-20 (NLT)
19 Understand this, my dear brothers and sisters: You must all be quick to listen, slow to speak, and slow to get angry.
20 Human anger does not produce the righteousness God desires.

JAMES 4:7 (ESV) Submit yourselves therefore to God. Resist the devil, and he will flee from you.

ROMANS 12:19-21 (NIV)

19 Do not take revenge, my dear friends, but leave room for God's wrath, for it is written: "It is mine to avenge; I will repay," says the Lord.

20 On the contrary: "If your enemy is hungry, feed him; if he is thirsty, give him something to drink. In doing this, you will heap burning coals on his head."

The Pocket Prayer

21 Do not be overcome by evil, but overcome evil with good.

NEHEMIAH 9:17 (NLT) They refused to obey and did not remember the miracles you had done for them. Instead, they became stubborn and appointed a leader to take them back to their slavery in Egypt. But you are a God of forgiveness, gracious and merciful, slow to become angry, and rich in unfailing love. You did not abandon them,

MATTHEW 5:22 (MSG) You're familiar with the command to the ancients, 'Do not murder.' I'm telling you that anyone who is so much as angry with a brother or sister is guilty of murder. Carelessly call a brother 'idiot!' and you just might find yourself hauled into court. Thoughtlessly yell 'stupid!' at a sister and you are on the brink of hellfire. The simple moral fact is that words kill.

DEUTERONOMY 32:35 (NLT) I will take revenge; I will pay them back. In due time their feet will slip. Their day of disaster will arrive, and their destiny will overtake them.

Authority

❧

GENESIS 1:28 (NIV) God blessed them and said to them, "Be fruitful and increase in number; fill the earth and subdue it. Rule over the fish in the sea and the birds in the sky and over every living creature that moves on the ground."

PSALM 18:29 (NLT) In your strength I can crush an army; with my God I can scale any wall.

PSALM 68:1 (NLT) Rise up, O God, and scatter your enemies. Let those who hate God run for their lives.

PSALM 91:7 (NKJV) A thousand may fall at your side, And ten thousand at your right hand; But it shall not come near you.

1 SAMUEL 2:10 (NLT) Those who fight against the LORD will be shattered. He thunders against them from heaven; the LORD judges throughout the earth. He gives power to his king; he increases the strength of his anointed one.

The Pocket Prayer

ISAIAH 54:17 (NLT) But in that coming day no weapon turned against you will succeed. You will silence every voice raised up to accuse you. These benefits are enjoyed by the servants of the LORD; their vindication will come from me. I, the LORD, have spoken!

ISAIAH 55:11 (ESV) so shall my word be that goes out from my mouth; it shall not return to me empty, but it shall accomplish that which I purpose, and shall succeed in the thing for which I sent it.

JOSHUA 1:5 (NLT) No one will be able to stand against you as long as you live. For I will be with you as I was with Moses. I will not fail you or abandon you.

MATTHEW 10:1 (NLT) Jesus called his twelve disciples together and gave them authority to cast out evil spirits and to heal every kind of disease and illness.

MATTHEW 11:12 (NKJV) And from the days of John the Baptist until now the kingdom of heaven suffers violence, and the violent take it by force.

MARK 11:23-24 (NKJV)

23 For assuredly, I say to you, whoever says to this mountain, 'Be removed and be cast into the sea,' and does not doubt in his heart, but believes that those things he says will be done, he will have whatever he says.

24 Therefore I say to you, whatever things you ask when you pray, believe that you receive them, and you will have them.

MARK 16:17-20 (NIV)

17 And these signs will accompany those who believe: In my name they will drive out demons; they will speak in new tongues;

18 they will pick up snakes with their hands; and when they drink deadly poison, it will not hurt them at all; they will place their hands on sick people, and they will get well.

19 After the Lord Jesus had spoken to them, he was taken up into heaven and he sat at the right hand of God.

20 Then the disciples went out and preached everywhere, and the Lord worked with them and confirmed his word by the signs that accompanied it.

LUKE 10:19 (ESV) Behold, I have given you authority to tread on serpents and scorpions, and over all the power of the enemy, and nothing shall hurt you.

JOHN 14:12-13 (NLT)
12 I tell you the truth, anyone who believes in me will do the same works I have done, and even greater works, because I am going to be with the Father.
13 You can ask for anything in my name, and I will do it, so that the Son can bring glory to the Father.

ROMANS 16:20 (HCSB) The God of peace will soon crush Satan under your feet. The grace of our Lord Jesus be with you.

ROMANS 8:31 (ESV) What then shall we say to these things? If God is for us, who can be against us?

EPHESIANS 1:20-22 (NIV)
20 he exerted when he raised Christ from the dead and seated him at his right hand in the heavenly realms,
21 far above all rule and authority, power and dominion, and every name that is

invoked, not only in the present age but also in the one to come.
22 And God placed all things under his feet and appointed him to be head over everything for the church,

EPHESIANS 2:6 (NASB) And God raised us up with Christ and seated us with him in the heavenly realms in Christ Jesus,

EPHESIANS 3:20 (NASB) Now to Him who is able to do far more abundantly beyond all that we ask or think, according to the power that works within us,

EPHESIANS 6:11-13 (NIV)
11 Put on the full armor of God, so that you can take your stand against the devil's schemes.
12 For our struggle is not against flesh and blood, but against the rulers, against the authorities, against the powers of this dark world and against the spiritual forces of evil in the heavenly realms.
13 Therefore put on the full armor of God, so that when the day of evil comes, you may be able to stand your ground, and after you have done everything, to stand.

The Pocket Prayer

1 CORINTHIANS 4:20 (NLT) For the Kingdom of God is not just a lot of talk; it is living by God's power.

2 CORINTHIANS 10:3-5 (NKJV)
3 For though we walk in the flesh, we do not war according to the flesh.
4 For the weapons of our warfare are not carnal but mighty in God for pulling down strongholds,
5 casting down arguments and every high thing that exalts itself against the knowledge of God, bringing every thought into captivity to the obedience of Christ,

COLOSSIANS 2:10 (NLT) So you also are complete through your union with Christ, who is the head over every ruler and authority.

COLOSSIANS 2:15 (NASB) When He had disarmed the rulers and authorities, He made a public display of them, having triumphed over them through Him.

JAMES 4:7 (NLT) So humble yourselves before God. Resist the devil, and he will flee from you.

1 JOHN 4:4 (TPT) Little children, you can be certain that you belong to God and have conquered them, for the One who is living in you is far greater than the one who is in the world.

1 JOHN 5:14-15 (NKJV)
14 Now this is the confidence that we have in Him, that if we ask anything according to His will, He hears us.
15 And if we know that He hears us, whatever we ask, we know that we have the petitions that we have asked of Him.

REVELATION 2:26 (NLT) To all who are victorious, who obey me to the very end, To them I will give authority over all the nations.

REVELATION 12:11 (ESV) And they have conquered him by the blood of the Lamb and by the word of their testimony, for they loved not their lives even unto death.

Battles of the Mind

❧

JOSHUA 1:8 (ESV) This Book of the Law shall not depart from your mouth, but you shall meditate on it day and night, so that you may be careful to do according to all that is written in it. For then you will make your way prosperous, and then you will have good success.

DEUTERONOMY 1:30-31 (NLT)
30 The LORD your God is going ahead of you. He will fight for you, just as you saw him do in Egypt.
31 And you saw how the LORD your God cared for you all along the way as you traveled through the wilderness, just as a father cares for his child. Now he has brought you to this place.

DEUTERONOMY 20:4 (NLT) For the LORD your God is going with you! He will fight for you against your enemies, and he will give you victory!

DEUTERONOMY 33:26 (NLT) There is no one like the God of Israel. He rides across the heavens to help you, across the skies in majestic splendor.

EXODUS 14:14 (NKJV) The LORD will fight for you, and you shall hold your peace.

PSALM 10:14 (HCSB) But You Yourself have seen trouble and grief, observing it in order to take the matter into Your hands. The helpless entrusts himself to You; You are a helper of the fatherless.

PSALM 55:22 (HCSB) Cast your burden on the LORD, and He will sustain you; He will never allow the righteous to be shaken.

PSALM 91:1-2 (NIV)
1 Whoever dwells in the shelter of the Most High will rest in the shadow of the Almighty.
2 I will say of the LORD, "He is my refuge and my fortress, my God, in whom I trust."

PSALM 121:2-8 (NIV)
2 My help comes from the LORD, the Maker of heaven and earth.

The Pocket Prayer

3 He will not let your foot slip—he who watches over you will not slumber;

4 indeed, he who watches over Israel will neither slumber nor sleep

5 The LORD watches over you— the LORD is your shade at your right hand;

6 the sun will not harm you by day, nor the moon by night.

7 The LORD will keep you from all harm— he will watch over your life;

8 the LORD will watch over your coming and going both now and forevermore.

PSALM 124:8 (TLB) Our help is from the Lord who made heaven and earth.

PSALM 145:14 (NLT) The LORD helps the fallen and lifts those bent beneath their loads.

PROVERBS 3:5-6 (NLT)

5 Trust in the LORD with all your heart; do not depend on your own understanding.

6 Seek his will in all you do, and he will show you which path to take.

PROVERBS 3:24-26 (NIV)
24 When you lie down, you will not be

afraid; when you lie down, your sleep will be sweet.
25 Have no fear of sudden disaster or of the ruin that overtakes the wicked,
26 for the LORD will be at your side and will keep your foot from being snared.

PROVERBS 19:21 (TPT) A person may have many ideas concerning God's plan for his life, but only the designs of his purpose will succeed in the end.

ISAIAH 55:8-9 (NKJV)
8 For My thoughts are not your thoughts, Nor are your ways My ways, says the LORD.
9 For as the heavens are higher than the earth, So are My ways higher than your ways, And My thoughts than your thoughts.

ISAIAH 26:3 (NKJV) You will keep him in perfect peace, whose mind is stayed on You, because he trusts in You.

MARK 4:24 (ESV) And he said to them, "Pay attention to what you hear: with the measure you use, it will be measured to you, and still more will be added to you."

JOHN 8:32 (TLB) and you will know the truth, and the truth will set you free.

EPHESIANS 3:16 (NLT) I pray that from his glorious, unlimited resources he will empower you with inner strength through his Spirit.

EPHESIANS 6:11-12 (NIV)
11 Put on the full armor of God, so that you can take your stand against the devil's schemes.
12 For our struggle is not against flesh and blood, but against the rulers, against the authorities, against the powers of this dark world and against the spiritual forces of evil in the heavenly realms.

ROMANS 12:2 (NLT) Don't copy the behavior and customs of this world, but let God transform you into a new person by changing the way you think. Then you will learn to know God's will for you, which is good and pleasing and perfect.

ROMANS 8:1-2 (ESV)
1 There is therefore now no condemnation for those who are in Christ Jesus.
2 For the law of the Spirit of life has set

you free in Christ Jesus from the law of sin and death.

ROMANS 8:26 (NLT) And the Holy Spirit helps us in our weakness. For example, we don't know what God wants us to pray for. But the Holy Spirit prays for us with groanings that cannot be expressed in words.

ROMANS 8:37 (NLT) No, despite all these things, overwhelming victory is ours through Christ, who loved us.

HEBREWS 4:16 (ESV) Let us then with confidence draw near to the throne of grace, that we may receive mercy and find grace to help in time of need.

1 CORINTHIANS 2:16 (NKJV) For "who has known the mind of the LORD that he may instruct Him?" But we have the mind of Christ.

2 CORINTHIANS 10:4 (NASB) for the weapons of our warfare are not of the flesh, but [a]divinely powerful for the destruction of fortresses.

The Pocket Prayer

1 PETER 5:7 (NIV) Cast all your anxiety on him because he cares for you.

2 TIMOTHY 1:7 (NKJV) For God has not given us a spirit of fear, but of power and of love and of a sound mind.

JAMES 4:6-7 (NIV)
6 But he gives us more grace. That is why Scripture says: "God opposes the proud but shows favor to the humble."
7 Submit yourselves, then, to God. Resist the devil, and he will flee from you.

JUDE 24-25 (NIV)
24 To him who is able to keep you from stumbling and to present you before his glorious presence without fault and with great joy,
25 to the only God our Savior be glory, majesty, power and authority, through Jesus Christ our Lord, before all ages, now and forevermore! Amen.

Blessing, Favor, Prosperity

≼

PHILIPPIANS 4:19 (NLT) And this same God who takes care of me will supply all your needs from his glorious riches, which have been given to us in Christ Jesus.

EPHESIANS 3:20 (NLT) Now all glory to God, who is able, through his mighty power at work within us, to accomplish infinitely more than we might ask or think.

JOHN 15:7 (NLT) But if you remain in me and my words remain in you, you may ask for anything you want, and it will be granted!

3 JOHN 2 (NKJV) Beloved, I pray that you may prosper in all things and be in health, just as your soul prospers.

2 CORINTHIANS 9:8 (NLT) And God will generously provide all you need. Then you will always have everything you need and plenty left over to share with others.

The Pocket Prayer

ISAIAH 1:19 (NIV) If you are willing and obedient, you will eat the good things of the land;

PSALM 35:27 (TLB) But give great joy to all who wish me well. Let them shout with delight, "Great is the Lord who enjoys helping his child!"

1 JOHN 5:14-15 (NKJV)
14 Now this is the confidence that we have in Him, that if we ask anything according to His will, He hears us.
15 And if we know that He hears us, whatever we ask, we know that we have the petitions that we have asked of Him.

2 CORINTHIANS 9:6-8 (NIV)
6 Remember this: Whoever sows sparingly will also reap sparingly, and whoever sows generously will also reap generously.
7 Each of you should give what you have decided in your heart to give, not reluctantly or under compulsion, for God loves a cheerful giver.
8 And God is able to bless you abundantly, so that in all things at all times, having all

that you need, you will abound in every good work.

PROVERBS 3:9 (NLT) Honor the Lord with your wealth and with the best part of everything you produce.

GALATIANS 3:13-14 (NIV)
13 Christ redeemed us from the curse of the law by becoming a curse for us, for it is written: "Cursed is everyone who is hung on a pole."
14 He redeemed us in order that the blessing given to Abraham might come to the Gentiles through Christ Jesus, so that by faith we might receive the promise of the Spirit.

PSALM 23:6 (NLT) Surely your goodness and unfailing love will pursue me all the days of my life, and I will live in the house of the Lord forever.

PROVERBS 24:3-4 (NKJV)
3 Through wisdom a house is built, and by understanding it is established;
4 By knowledge the rooms are filled with all precious and pleasant riches.

The Pocket Prayer

PSALM 112:2-3 (NKJV)
2 His descendants will be mighty on earth; The generation of the upright will be blessed.
3 Wealth and riches will be in his house, and his righteousness endures forever.

PSALM 23:1 (TLB) Because the Lord is my Shepherd, I have everything I need!

PSALM 34:10 (ESV) The young lions suffer want and hunger; but those who seek the Lord lack no good thing.

JOSHUA 1:8 (NLT) Study this Book of Instruction continually. Meditate on it day and night so you will be sure to obey everything written in it. Only then will you prosper and succeed in all you do.

PROVERBS 13:22 (HCSB) A good man leaves an inheritance to his grandchildren, but the sinner's wealth is stored up for the righteous.

MATTHEW 6:33 (NKJV) But seek first the kingdom of God and His righteousness, and all these things shall be added to you.

ISAIAH 55:11 (NKJV) So shall My word be that goes forth from My mouth; It shall not return to Me void, But it shall accomplish what I please, And it shall prosper in the thing for which I sent it.

PROVERBS 10:4 (TLB) Lazy men are soon poor; hard workers get rich.

DEUTERONOMY 28:6-8 (NIV)
6 You will be blessed when you come in and blessed when you go out.
7 The LORD will grant that the enemies who rise up against you will be defeated before you. They will come at you from one direction but flee from you in seven.
8 The LORD will send a blessing on your barns and on everything you put your hand to. The LORD your God will bless you in the land he is giving you.

LUKE 6:38 (ESV) Give, and it will be given to you. good measure, pressed down, shaken together, running over, will be put into your lap. For with the measure you use, it will be measured back to you.

MALACHI 3:10 (ESV) Bring the full tithe into the storehouse, that there may

The Pocket Prayer

be food in my house. And thereby put me to the test, says the Lord of hosts, if I will not open the windows of heaven for you and pour down for you a blessing until there is no more need.

PSALM 5:12 (HCSB) For You, Lord, bless the righteous one; You surround him with favor like a shield.

PROVERBS 10:22 (ESV) The blessing of the Lord makes rich, and he adds no sorrow with it.

PSALM 112:5 (NLT) Good comes to those who lend money generously and conduct their business fairly.

HAGGAI 2:8 (NLT) The silver is mine, and the gold is mine, says the Lord of Heaven's Armies.

DEUTERONOMY 1:11 (NLT) And may the LORD, the God of your ancestors, multiply you a thousand times more and bless you as he promised!

GALATIANS 6:7 (NKJV) Do not be deceived, God is not mocked; for whatever a man sows, that he will also reap.

MARK 4:8 (TLV) And others fell into the good soil and were producing fruit, springing up and increasing. They yielded a crop, producing thirty, sixty, and a hundredfold.

Children

∽

PSALM 8:2 (NLT) You have taught children and infants to tell of your strength, silencing your enemies and all who oppose you.

PSALM 113:9 (NLT) He gives the childless woman a family, making her a happy mother. Praise the LORD!

PSALM 127:3-5 (NLT)
3 Children are a gift from the LORD; they are a reward from him.
4 Children born to a young man are like arrows in a warrior's hands.
5 How joyful is the man whose quiver is full of them!

PSALM 139:13-16 (NIV)
13 For you created my inmost being; you knit me together in my mother's womb.
14 I praise you because I am fearfully and wonderfully made; your works are wonderful, I know that full well.
15 My frame was not hidden from you when I was made in the secret place,

when I was woven together in the depths of the earth.
16 Your eyes saw my unformed body; all the days ordained for me were written in your book before one of them came to be.

ISAIAH 54:13 (NIV) All your children will be taught by the LORD, and great will be their peace.

DEUTERONOMY 11:19 (TLV) You are to teach them to your children, speaking of them when you sit in your house, when you walk by the way, when you lie down and when you rise up.

EXODUS 20:12 (NIV) Honor your father and your mother, so that you may live long in the land the LORD your God is giving you.

PROVERBS 1:8-9 (NIV)
8 Listen, my son, to your father's instruction and do not forsake your mother's teaching.
9 They are a garland to grace your head and a chain to adorn your neck.

PROVERBS 13:24 (NIV) Whoever spares the rod hates their children, but the one who loves their children is careful to discipline them.

PROVERBS 17:6 (NIV) Children's children are a crown to the aged, and parents are the pride of their children.

PROVERBS 22:6 (NKJV) Train up a child in the way he should go, And when he is old he will not depart from it.

PROVERBS 22:15 (NLT) A youngster's heart is filled with foolishness, but physical discipline will drive it far away.

JEREMIAH 29:11 (NIV) "For I know the plans I have for you," declares the LORD, "plans to prosper you and not to harm you, plans to give you hope and a future."

MATTHEW 18:2-5 (NIV)
2 He called a little child to him, and placed the child among them.
3 And he said: "Truly I tell you, unless you change and become like little children, you will never enter the kingdom of heaven.
4 Therefore, whoever takes the lowly

position of this child is the greatest in the kingdom of heaven.

5 And whoever welcomes one such child in my name welcomes me.

MATTHEW 18:10 (NLT) Beware that you don't look down on any of these little ones. For I tell you that in heaven their angels are always in the presence of my heavenly Father.

MARK 9:36-37 (NLT)
36 Then he put a little child among them. Taking the child in his arms, he said to them,
37 "Anyone who welcomes a little child like this on my behalf welcomes me, and anyone who welcomes me welcomes not only me but also my Father who sent me."

MARK 10:14 (NLT) When Jesus saw what was happening, he was angry with his disciples. He said to them, "Let the children come to me. Don't stop them! For the Kingdom of God belongs to those who are like these children.

ACTS 17:28 (NASB) for in Him we live and move and exist, as even some of your own poets have said, 'For we also are His children.'

EPHESIANS 1:4-5 (NIV)
4 For he chose us in him before the creation of the world to be holy and blameless in his sight. in love
5 He predestined us for adoption to sonship through Jesus Christ, in accordance with his pleasure and will.

EPHESIANS 1:11 (NIV) In him we were also chosen, having been predestined according to the plan of him who works out everything in conformity with the purpose of his will,

EPHESIANS 6:1-4 (NIV)
1 Children, obey your parents in the Lord, for this is right.
2 "Honor your father and mother"—which is the first commandment with a promise—
3 "so that it may go well with you and that you may enjoy long life on the earth."
4 Fathers, do not exasperate your children; instead, bring them up in the training and instruction of the Lord.

COLOSSIANS 3:20 (NIV) Children, obey your parents in everything, for this pleases the Lord.

ROMANS 8:29-30 (NIV)
29 For those God foreknew he also predestined to be conformed to the image of his Son, that he might be the firstborn among many brothers and sisters.
30 And those he predestined, he also called; those he called, he also justified; those he justified, he also glorified.

1 TIMOTHY 4:12 (NIV) Don't let anyone look down on you because you are young, but set an example for the believers in speech, in conduct, in love, in faith and in purity.

1 PETER 2:9 (NIV) But you are a chosen people, a royal priesthood, a holy nation, God's special possession, that you may declare the praises of him who called you out of darkness into his wonderful light.

JAMES 1:17 (NIV) Every good and perfect gift is from above, coming down from the Father of the heavenly

The Pocket Prayer

lights, who does not change like shifting shadows.

3 JOHN 4 (NIV) I have no greater joy than to hear that my children are walking in the truth.

Depression

◈

PSALM 40:2 (NLT) He lifted me out of the pit of despair, out of the mud and the mire. He set my feet on solid ground and steadied me as I walked along.

PSALM 34:18 (NLT) The LORD is close to the brokenhearted; he rescues those whose spirits are crushed.

PHILIPPIANS 4:13 (NKJV) I can do all things through Christ who strengthens me.

PSALM 112:4 (TLV) Light shines in the darkness for the upright. Gracious, compassionate and just is he.

PSALM 40:9-10 (NIV)
9 I proclaim your saving acts in the great assembly; I do not seal my lips, LORD, as you know.
10 I do not hide your righteousness in my heart; I speak of your faithfulness and your saving help. I do not conceal your love and your faithfulness from the great assembly.

The Pocket Prayer

PSALM 43:4-5 (NLT)
4 There I will go to the altar of God, to God—the source of all my joy. I will praise you with my harp, O God, my God!
5 Why am I discouraged? Why is my heart so sad? I will put my hope in God! I will praise him again—my Savior and my God!

JEREMIAH 1:19 (NLT) They will fight you, but they will fail. For I am with you, and I will take care of you. I, the LORD, have spoken!

DEUTERONOMY 31:8 (NKJV) And the LORD, He is the One who goes before you. He will be with you, He will not leave you nor forsake you; do not fear nor be dismayed.

ROMANS 8:18-19 (NKJV)
18 For I consider that the sufferings of this present time are not worthy to be compared with the glory which shall be revealed in us.
19 For the earnest expectation of the creation eagerly waits for the revealing of the sons of God.

PROVERBS 15:13 (TLV) A joyful heart makes the face cheerful, but heartache crushes the spirit.

ROMANS 12:2 (TLV) Do not be conformed to this world but be transformed by the renewing of your mind, so that you may discern what is the will of God—what is good and acceptable and perfect.

PSALM 23:4 (NLT) Even when I walk through the darkest valley, I will not be afraid, for you are close beside me. Your rod and your staff protect and comfort me.

PHILIPPIANS 4:6-7 (NASB)
6 Be anxious for nothing, but in everything by prayer and supplication with thanksgiving let your requests be made known to God.
7 And the peace of God, which surpasses all comprehension, will guard your hearts and your minds in Christ Jesus.

JOHN 10:10 (NASB) The thief comes only to steal and kill and destroy; I came

The Pocket Prayer

that they may have life, and have it abundantly.

MATTHEW 6:33 (HCSB) But seek first the kingdom of God and His righteousness, and all these things will be provided for you.

PSALM 30:11 (NLT) You have turned my mourning into joyful dancing. You have taken away my clothes of mourning and clothed me with joy,

PSALM 9:9 (NLT) The LORD is a shelter for the oppressed, a refuge in times of trouble.

ISAIAH 40:31 (NLT) But those who trust in the LORD will find new strength. They will soar high on wings like eagles. They will run and not grow weary. They will walk and not faint.

PSALM 3:3 (ESV) But You, LORD, are a shield around me, my glory, and the One who lifts up my head

2 TIMOTHY 1:7 (NLT) For God has not given us a spirit of fear and timidity, but of power, love, and self-discipline.

1 PETER 1:13 (NLT) So prepare your minds for action and exercise self-control. Put all your hope in the gracious salvation that will come to you when Jesus Christ is revealed to the world.

2 CORINTHIANS 7:10 (ESV) But You, LORD, are a shield around me, my glory, and the One who lifts up my head.

PROVERBS 12:25 (HCSB) Anxiety in a man's heart weighs it down, but a good word cheers it up.

ISAIAH 26:3 (TLV) You keep in perfect peace one whose mind is stayed on You, because he trusts in You.

ROMANS 15:13 (NLT) I pray that God, the source of hope, will fill you completely with joy and peace because you trust in him. Then you will overflow with confident hope through the power of the Holy Spirit.

PSALM 103:1-5 (NIV)
1 Praise the LORD, my soul; all my inmost being, praise his holy name.
2 Praise the LORD, my soul, and forget not all his benefits—

The Pocket Prayer

3 Who forgives all your sins and heals all your diseases,
4 Who redeems your life from the pit and crowns you with love and compassion,
5 Who satisfies your desires with good things so that your youth is renewed like the eagle's.

PHILIPPIANS 4:8 (NIV) Finally, brothers and sisters, whatever is true, whatever is noble, whatever is right, whatever is pure, whatever is lovely, whatever is admirable—if anything is excellent or praiseworthy—think about such things.

2 CORINTHIANS 10:4-5 (NIV)
4 The weapons we fight with are not the weapons of the world. On the contrary, they have divine power to demolish strongholds.
5 We demolish arguments and every pretension that sets itself up against the knowledge of God, and we take captive every thought to make it obedient to Christ.

Faith

❦

MARK 11:22-24 (NIV)
22 "Have faith in God," Jesus answered.
23 "Truly I tell you, if anyone says to this mountain, 'Go, throw yourself into the sea,' and does not doubt in their heart but believes that what they say will happen, it will be done for them.
24 Therefore I tell you, whatever you ask for in prayer, believe that you have received it, and it will be yours.

1 CORINTHIANS 2:5 (NLT) I did this so you would trust not in human wisdom but in the power of God.

PHILEMON 1:6 (NLT) And I am praying that you will put into action the generosity that comes from your faith as you understand and experience all the good things we have in Christ.

HEBREWS 11:1 (NKJV) Now faith is the substance of things hoped for, the evidence of things not seen.

The Pocket Prayer

MATTHEW 21:22 (ESV) And whatever you ask in prayer, you will receive, if you have faith."

ROMANS 10:17 (NKJV) So then faith comes by hearing, and hearing by the word of God.

EPHESIANS 2:8-9 (ESV)
8 For by grace you have been saved through faith. And this is not your own doing; it is the gift of God,
9 not a result of works, so that no one may boast.

LUKE 1:37 (TPT) Not one promise from God is empty of power, for nothing is impossible with God!

PROVERBS 3:5-6 (NKJV)
5 Trust in the LORD with all your heart, And lean not on your own understanding;
6 In all your ways acknowledge Him, And He shall direct your paths.

2 CORINTHIANS 5:7 (NKJV) For we walk by faith, not by sight.

HEBREWS 10:23-24 (NLT)
23 Let us hold tightly without wavering

to the hope we affirm, for God can be trusted to keep his promise.

24 Let us think of ways to motivate one another to acts of love and good works.

HEBREWS 11:6 (NLT) And it is impossible to please God without faith. Anyone who wants to come to him must believe that God exists and that he rewards those who sincerely seek him.

JAMES 1:5-8 (NIV)
5 If any of you lacks wisdom, you should ask God, who gives generously to all without finding fault, and it will be given to you.
6 But when you ask, you must believe and not doubt, because the one who doubts is like a wave of the sea, blown and tossed by the wind.
7 That person should not expect to receive anything from the Lord.
8 Such a person is double-minded and unstable in all they do.

JAMES 2:17 (ESV) So also faith by itself, if it does not have works, is dead.

The Pocket Prayer

JAMES 2:22 (ESV) You see that faith was active along with his works, and faith was completed by his works;

ROMANS 12:3 (NIV) For by the grace given me I say to every one of you: Do not think of yourself more highly than you ought, but rather think of yourself with sober judgment, in accordance with the faith God has distributed to each of you.

ROMANS 5:1-2 (NLT)
1Therefore, since we have been made right in God's sight by faith, we have peace with God because of what Jesus Christ our Lord has done for us.
2 Because of our faith, Christ has brought us into this place of undeserved privilege where we now stand, and we confidently and joyfully look forward to sharing God's glory.

PSALM 46:10 (NLT) Be still, and know that I am God! I will be honored by every nation. I will be honored throughout the world.

MARK 9:23 (NLT) "What do you mean, 'If I can'?" Jesus asked. "Anything is possible if a person believes."

MATTHEW 21:21-22 (NLT)
21 Then Jesus told them, "I tell you the truth, if you have faith and don't doubt, you can do things like this and much more. You can even say to this mountain, 'May you be lifted up and thrown into the sea,' and it will happen.
22 You can pray for anything, and if you have faith, you will receive it."

MATTHEW 17:20 (NLT) "You don't have enough faith," Jesus told them. "I tell you the truth, if you had faith even as small as a mustard seed, you could say to this mountain, 'Move from here to there,' and it would move. Nothing would be impossible."

COLOSSIANS 2:6-7 (NKJV)
6 As you therefore have received Christ Jesus the Lord, so walk in Him,
7 rooted and built up in Him and established in the faith, as you have been taught, abounding in it with thanksgiving.

The Pocket Prayer

HABAKKUK 2:4 (NLT) Look at the proud! They trust in themselves, and their lives are crooked. But the righteous will live by their faithfulness to God.

2 CORINTHIANS 4:13 (NLT) But we continue to preach because we have the same kind of faith the psalmist had when he said, "I believed in God, so I spoke."

Fear, Anxiety

⌇

2 TIMOTHY 1:7 (NKJV) For God has not given us a spirit of fear, but of power and of love and of a sound mind.

MATTHEW 28:20 (NLT) Teach these new disciples to obey all the commands I have given you. And be sure of this: I am with you always, even to the end of the age.

DEUTERONOMY 1:29-31 (NIV)
29 Then I said to you, "Do not be terrified; do not be afraid of them.
30 The LORD your God, who is going before you, will fight for you, as he did for you in Egypt, before your very eyes,
31 and in the wilderness. There you saw how the LORD your God carried you, as a father carries his son, all the way you went until you reached this place."

PSALM 3:6-7 (NLT)
6 I am not afraid of ten thousand enemies who surround me on every side.
7 Arise, O LORD! Rescue me, my God!

The Pocket Prayer

Slap all my enemies in the face! Shatter the teeth of the wicked!

PSALM 27:1 (NLT) The LORD is my light and my salvation— so why should I be afraid? The LORD is my fortress, protecting me from danger, so why should I tremble?

PSALM 27:5 (NLT) For he will conceal me there when troubles come; he will hide me in his sanctuary. He will place me out of reach on a high rock.

PSALM 56:4 (TPT) What harm could a man bring to me? With God on my side I will not be afraid of what comes. The roaring praises of God fill my heart, and I will always triumph as I trust his promises.

PSALM 91 (NIV)
1 Whoever dwells in the shelter of the Most High will rest in the shadow of the Almighty.
2 I will say of the LORD, "He is my refuge and my fortress, my God, in whom I trust."

3 Surely he will save you from the fowler's snare and from the deadly pestilence.

4 He will cover you with his feathers, and under his wings you will find refuge; his faithfulness will be your shield and rampart.

5 You will not fear the terror of night, nor the arrow that flies by day,

6 nor the pestilence that stalks in the darkness, nor the plague that destroys at midday.

7 A thousand may fall at your side, ten thousand at your right hand, but it will not come near you.

8 You will only observe with your eyes and see the punishment of the wicked.

9 If you say, "The LORD is my refuge," and you make the Most High your dwelling,

10 no harm will overtake you, no disaster will come near your tent.

11 For he will command his angels concerning you to guard you in all your ways;

12 they will lift you up in their hands, so that you will not strike your foot against a stone.

13 You will tread on the lion and the

cobra; you will trample the great lion and the serpent.

14 "Because he loves me," says the LORD, "I will rescue him; I will protect him, for he acknowledges my name.

15 He will call on me, and I will answer him; I will be with him in trouble, I will deliver him and honor him.

16 With long life I will satisfy him and show him my salvation."

PROVERBS 3:24-26 (NLT)
24 You can go to bed without fear; you will lie down and sleep soundly.

25 You need not be afraid of sudden disaster or the destruction that comes upon the wicked,

26 for the LORD is your security. He will keep your foot from being caught in a trap.

JOSHUA 1:9 (NLT) This is my command—be strong and courageous! Do not be afraid or discouraged. For the LORD your God is with you wherever you go.

ISAIAH 41:10 (NASB) Do not fear, for I am with you; Do not anxiously look about you, for I am your God. I will strengthen you, surely I will help you, Surely I will uphold you with My righteous right hand.

ISAIAH 43:1 (NLT) But now, O Jacob, listen to the LORD who created you. O Israel, the one who formed you says, "Do not be afraid, for I have ransomed you. I have called you by name; you are mine."

1 JOHN 4:18 (NLT) Such love has no fear, because perfect love expels all fear. If we are afraid, it is for fear of punishment, and this shows that we have not fully experienced his perfect love.

PHILIPPIANS 4:6 (TLV) Do not be anxious about anything—but in everything, by prayer and petition with thanksgiving, let your requests be made known to God.

1 PETER 5:6-7 (NASB)
6 Therefore humble yourselves under the mighty hand of God, that He may exalt you at the proper time,
7 casting all your anxiety on Him, because He cares for you.

The Pocket Prayer

MATTHEW 6:26-27, 30 (NIV)
26 Look at the birds of the air; they do not sow or reap or store away in barns, and yet your heavenly Father feeds them. Are you not much more valuable than they?
27 Can any one of you by worrying add a single hour to your life?
30 If that is how God clothes the grass of the field, which is here today and tomorrow is thrown into the fire, will he not much more clothe you—you of little faith?

ISAIAH 35:4 (NASB) Say to those with anxious heart, "Take courage, fear not. Behold, your God will come with vengeance; The recompense of God will come, But He will save you."

JOHN 14:27 (TLB) I am leaving you with a gift—peace of mind and heart! And the peace I give isn't fragile like the peace the world gives. So don't be troubled or afraid.

PSALM 23:4 (ESV) Even though I walk through the valley of the shadow of death, I will fear no evil, for you are with me; your rod and your staff, they comfort me.

PSALM 34:4 (NASB) I sought the LORD, and He answered me, And delivered me from all my fears.

PSALM 94:19 (NASB) When my anxious thoughts multiply within me, Your consolations delight my soul.

ROMANS 8:38-39 (NIV)
38 For I am convinced that neither death nor life, neither angels nor demons, neither the present nor the future, nor any powers,
39 neither height nor depth, nor anything else in all creation, will be able to separate us from the love of God that is in Christ Jesus our Lord.

PSALM 115:11 (NLT) All you who fear the LORD, trust the LORD! He is your helper and your shield.

DEUTERONOMY 31:6 (NLT) So be strong and courageous! Do not be afraid and do not panic before them. For the LORD your God will personally go ahead of you. He will neither fail you nor abandon you.

The Pocket Prayer

ISAIAH 41:13 (NKJV) For I, the LORD your God, will hold your right hand, saying to you, 'Fear not, I will help you.'

1 CORINTHIANS 16:13 (NLT) Be on guard. Stand firm in the faith. Be courageous. Be strong.

Forgiveness, Offense, Bitterness

※

PROVERBS 19:11 (NLT) Sensible people control their temper; they earn respect by overlooking wrongs.

ECCLESIASTES 7:21-22 (NASB)
21 Also, do not take seriously all words which are spoken, so that you will not hear your servant cursing you.
22 For you also have realized that you likewise have many times cursed others.

MATTHEW 18:15-17 (NIV)
15 If your brother or sister sins, go and point out their fault, just between the two of you. If they listen to you, you have won them over.
16 But if they will not listen, take one or two others along, so that 'every matter may be established by the testimony of two or three witnesses.'
17 If they still refuse to listen, tell it to the church; and if they refuse to listen even to the church, treat them as you would a pagan or a tax collector.

The Pocket Prayer

LUKE 17:3-4 (NASB)
3 "Be on your guard! If your brother sins, rebuke him; and if he repents, forgive him.
4 And if he sins against you seven times a day, and returns to you seven times, saying, 'I repent,' forgive him."

JAMES 3:16 (NLT) For wherever there is jealousy and selfish ambition, there you will find disorder and evil of every kind.

EPHESIANS 4:2-3 (NLT)
2 Always be humble and gentle. Be patient with each other, making allowance for each other's faults because of your love.
3 Make every effort to keep yourselves united in the Spirit, binding yourselves together with peace.

EPHESIANS 5:1-2 (NLT)
1 Imitate God, therefore, in everything you do, because you are his dear children.
2 Live a life filled with love, following the example of Christ. He loved us and offered himself as a sacrifice for us, a pleasing aroma to God.

LEVITICUS 19:18 (NKJV) You shall not take vengeance, nor bear any grudge against the children of your people, but you shall love your neighbor as yourself: I am the LORD.

1 CORINTHIANS 13:4-6 (ESV)
4 Love is patient and kind; love does not envy or boast; it is not arrogant
5 or rude. It does not insist on its own way; it is not irritable or resentful;
6 it does not rejoice at wrongdoing, but rejoices with the truth.

1 PETER 2:22-23 (TLB)
22 He never sinned, never told a lie,
23 never answered back when insulted; when he suffered he did not threaten to get even; he left his case in the hands of God who always judges fairly.

MATTHEW 7:1-2 (NASB)
1 Do not judge so that you will not be judged.
2 For in the way you judge, you will be judged; and by your standard of measure, it will be measured to you.

The Pocket Prayer

JAMES 1:19 (TPT) My dearest brothers and sisters, take this to heart: Be quick to listen, but slow to speak. And be slow to become angry,

GALATIANS 6:1-3 (NIV)
1 Brothers and sisters, if someone is caught in a sin, you who live by the Spirit should restore that person gently. But watch yourselves, or you also may be tempted.
2 Carry each other's burdens, and in this way you will fulfill the law of Christ.
3 If anyone thinks they are something when they are not, they deceive themselves.

ACTS 24:16 (NLT) Because of this, I always try to maintain a clear conscience before God and all people.

EPHESIANS 4:26 (NLT) And "don't sin by letting anger control you." Don't let the sun go down while you are still angry,

PROVERBS 17:9 (HCSB) Whoever conceals an offense promotes love, but whoever gossips about it separates friends.

EPHESIANS 4:32 (HCSB) And be kind and compassionate to one another, forgiving one another, just as God also forgave you in Christ.

PROVERBS 10:12 (ESV) Hatred stirs up strife, but love covers all offenses.

GALATIANS 5:22-23 (NIV)
22 But the fruit of the Spirit is love, joy, peace, forbearance, kindness, goodness, faithfulness,
23 gentleness and self-control. Against such things there is no law.

GALATIANS 5:26 (NKJV) Let us not become conceited, provoking one another, envying one another.

COLOSSIANS 3:13 (NKJV) bearing with one another, and forgiving one another, if anyone has a complaint against another; even as Christ forgave you, so you also must do.

HEBREWS 12:15 (NLT) Look after each other so that none of you fails to receive the grace of God. Watch out that no poisonous root of bitterness grows up to trouble you, corrupting many.

MATTHEW 11:6 (NKJV) And blessed is he who is not offended because of Me.

ISAIAH 44:22 (NLT) I have swept away your sins like a cloud. I have scattered your offenses like the morning mist. Oh, return to me, for I have paid the price to set you free.

2 TIMOTHY 2:23-24 (NIV)
23 Don't have anything to do with foolish and stupid arguments, because you know they produce quarrels.
24 And the Lord's servant must not be quarrelsome but must be kind to everyone, able to teach, not resentful.

Guidance, Led by the Spirit

◈

PSALM 23:1-3 (NIV)
1 The LORD is my shepherd, I lack nothing.
2 He makes me lie down in green pastures, he leads me beside quiet waters,
3 He refreshes my soul. He guides me along the right paths for his name's sake.

PSALM 25:4-5 (NLT)
4 Show me the right path, O LORD; point out the road for me to follow.
5 Lead me by your truth and teach me, for you are the God who saves me. All day long I put my hope in you.

PSALM 31:3 (NKJV) For You are my rock and my fortress; Therefore, for Your name's sake, Lead me and guide me.

PSALM 32:8 (NKJV) I will instruct you and teach you in the way you should go; I will guide you with My eye.

PSALM 37:23 (NKJV) The steps of a good man are ordered by the LORD, And He delights in his way.

The Pocket Prayer

ROMANS 9:1 (NLT) With Christ as my witness, I speak with utter truthfulness. My conscience and the Holy Spirit confirm it.

JEREMIAH 29:13 (ESV) You will seek me and find me, when you seek me with all your heart.

1 THESSALONIANS 5:17 (ESV) Pray without ceasing,

COLOSSIANS 1:9-10 (NIV)
9 For this reason, since the day we heard about you, we have not stopped praying for you. We continually ask God to fill you with the knowledge of his will through all the wisdom and understanding that the Spirit gives,
10 so that you may live a life worthy of the Lord and please him in every way: bearing fruit in every good work, growing in the knowledge of God,

EPHESIANS 1:17-18 (HCSB)
17 I pray that the God of our Lord Jesus Christ, the glorious Father, would give you a spirit of wisdom and revelation in the knowledge of Him.

18 I pray that the perception of your mind may be enlightened so you may know what is the hope of His calling, what are the glorious riches of His inheritance among the saints,

EPHESIANS 6:10-18 (NIV)

10 Finally, be strong in the Lord and in his mighty power.

11 Put on the full armor of God, so that you can take your stand against the devil's schemes.

12 For our struggle is not against flesh and blood, but against the rulers, against the authorities, against the powers of this dark world and against the spiritual forces of evil in the heavenly realms.

13 Therefore put on the full armor of God, so that when the day of evil comes, you may be able to stand your ground, and after you have done everything, to stand.

14 Stand firm then, with the belt of truth buckled around your waist, with the breastplate of righteousness in place,

15 and with your feet fitted with the readiness that comes from the gospel of peace.

16 In addition to all this, take up the shield

The Pocket Prayer

of faith, with which you can extinguish all the flaming arrows of the evil one.

17 Take the helmet of salvation and the sword of the Spirit, which is the word of God.

18 And pray in the Spirit on all occasions with all kinds of prayers and requests. With this in mind, be alert and always keep on praying for all the Lord's people.

HEBREWS 4:16 (NKJV) Let us therefore come boldly to the throne of grace, that we may obtain mercy and find grace to help in time of need.

PSALM 73:23-24 (NLT)
23 Yet I still belong to you; you hold my right hand.
24 You guide me with your counsel, leading me to a glorious destiny.

PSALM 119:105 (NLT) Your word is a lamp to guide my feet and a light for my path.

PROVERBS 3:5-6 (NLT)
5 Trust in the LORD with all your heart; do not depend on your own understanding.

6 Seek his will in all you do, and he will show you which path to take.

PROVERBS 16:3 (TLB) Commit your work to the Lord, then it will succeed.

PROVERBS 23:19 (TPT) As you listen to me, my beloved child, you will grow in wisdom and your heart will be drawn into understanding, which will empower you to make right decisions.

ISAIAH 30:21 (TPT) When you turn to the right or turn to the left, you will hear his voice behind you to guide you, saying, "This is the right path; follow it."

JOHN 16:13 (NLT) When the Spirit of truth comes, he will guide you into all truth. He will not speak on his own but will tell you what he has heard. He will tell you about the future.

ISAIAH 26:3 (NLT) You will keep in perfect peace all who trust in you, all whose thoughts are fixed on you!

2 SAMUEL 22:33 (TLB) I knew his laws, And I obeyed them.

The Pocket Prayer

JOHN 15:4-5 (NIV)

4 Remain in me, as I also remain in you. No branch can bear fruit by itself; it must remain in the vine. Neither can you bear fruit unless you remain in me.

5 "I am the vine; you are the branches. If you remain in me and I in you, you will bear much fruit; apart from me you can do nothing.

JOHN 15:7-8 (NASB)

7 If you abide in Me, and My words abide in you, ask whatever you wish, and it will be done for you.

8 My Father is glorified by this, that you bear much fruit, and so prove to be My disciples.

JAMES 4:7-8 (NASB)

7 Submit therefore to God. Resist the devil and he will flee from you.

8 Draw near to God and He will draw near to you. Cleanse your hands, you sinners; and purify your hearts, you double-minded.

JOHN 16:23-24 (NKJV)

23 And in that day you will ask Me nothing. Most assuredly, I say to you,

whatever you ask the Father in My name He will give you.

24 Until now you have asked nothing in My name. Ask, and you will receive, that your joy may be full.

ISAIAH 48:17 (HCSB) This is what the LORD, your Redeemer, the Holy One of Israel says: I am Yahweh your God, who teaches you for your benefit, who leads you in the way you should go.

Healing

∽

EXODUS 15:26 (NLT) He said, "If you will listen carefully to the voice of the LORD your God and do what is right in his sight, obeying his commands and keeping all his decrees, then I will not make you suffer any of the diseases I sent on the Egyptians; for I am the LORD who heals you."

DEUTERONOMY 30:19-20 (NIV)
19 This day I call the heavens and the earth as witnesses against you that I have set before you life and death, blessings and curses. Now choose life, so that you and your children may live,
20 and that you may love the LORD your God, listen to his voice, and hold fast to him. For the LORD is your life, and he will give you many years in the land he swore to give to your fathers, Abraham, Isaac and Jacob.

PSALM 103:3 (NLT) He forgives all my sins and heals all my diseases.

Pamela Christian Flickinger

PSALM 107:20 (ESV) He sent out his word and healed them, and delivered them from their destruction.

PROVERBS 4:20-22 (ESV)
20 My son, be attentive to my words; incline your ear to my sayings.
21 Let them not escape from your sight; keep them within your heart.
22 For they are life to those who find them, and healing to all their flesh.

ISAIAH 41:10 (NKJV) Fear not, for I am with you; Be not dismayed, for I am your God. I will strengthen you, Yes, I will help you, I will uphold you with My righteous right hand.

ISAIAH 53:4-5 (NIV)
4 Surely he took up our pain and bore our suffering, yet we considered him punished by God, stricken by him, and afflicted.
5 But he was pierced for our transgressions, he was crushed for our iniquities; the punishment that brought us peace was on him, and by his wounds we are healed.

JEREMIAH 30:17 (NASB) 'For I will restore you to health And I will heal you of your wounds,' declares the LORD, 'Because they have called you an outcast, saying: "It is Zion; no one cares for her."'

JEREMIAH 32:27 (NASB) "Behold, I am the LORD, the God of all flesh; is anything too difficult for Me?"

JOEL 3:10 (NLT) Hammer your plowshares into swords and your pruning hooks into spears. Train even your weaklings to be warriors.

MATTHEW 18:18-19 (NLT)
18 "I tell you the truth, whatever you forbid on earth will be forbidden in heaven, and whatever you permit on earth will be permitted in heaven.
19 "I also tell you this: If two of you agree here on earth concerning anything you ask, my Father in heaven will do it for you."

MATTHEW 21:21-22 (HCSB)
21 Jesus answered them, "I assure you: If you have faith and do not doubt, you will not only do what was done to the fig

tree, but even if you tell this mountain, 'Be lifted up and thrown into the sea,' it will be done.

22 And if you believe, you will receive whatever you ask for in prayer."

MARK 9:23 (HCSB) Then Jesus said to him, "'If You can'? Everything is possible to the one who believes."

MARK 16:15-18 (NIV)
15 He said to them, "Go into all the world and preach the gospel to all creation.
16 Whoever believes and is baptized will be saved, but whoever does not believe will be condemned.
17 And these signs will accompany those who believe: In my name they will drive out demons; they will speak in new tongues;
18 they will pick up snakes with their hands; and when they drink deadly poison, it will not hurt them at all; they will place their hands on sick people, and they will get well."

ROMANS 4:19-21 (NKJV)
19 And not being weak in faith, he did not consider his own body, already dead

The Pocket Prayer

(since he was about a hundred years old), and the deadness of Sarah's womb.

20 He did not waver at the promise of God through unbelief, but was strengthened in faith, giving glory to God,

21 and being fully convinced that what He had promised He was also able to perform.

ROMANS 8:11 (NLT) The Spirit of God, who raised Jesus from the dead, lives in you. And just as God raised Christ Jesus from the dead, he will give life to your mortal bodies by this same Spirit living within you.

2 CORINTHIANS 4:13 (NLT) But we continue to preach because we have the same kind of faith the psalmist had when he said, "I believed in God, so I spoke."

2 CORINTHIANS 4:18 (NLT) So we don't look at the troubles we can see now; rather, we fix our gaze on things that cannot be seen. For the things we see now will soon be gone, but the things we cannot see will last forever.

GALATIANS 3:29 (NKJV) And if you are Christ's, then you are Abraham's seed, and heirs according to the promise.

PHILIPPIANS 2:13 (NLT) For God is working in you, giving you the desire and the power to do what pleases him.

HEBREWS 10:23 (NASB) Let us hold fast the confession of our hope without wavering, for He who promised is faithful;

HEBREWS 13:8 (NASB) Jesus Christ is the same yesterday and today and forever.

JAMES 4:7 (NLT) So humble yourselves before God. Resist the devil, and he will flee from you.

1 PETER 2:24 (NKJV) Who Himself bore our sins in His own body on the tree, that we, having died to sins, might live for righteousness—by whose [a]stripes you were healed.

1 JOHN 3:21-22 (NKJV)
21 Beloved, if our heart does not condemn us, we have confidence toward God.
22 And whatever we ask we receive

The Pocket Prayer

from Him, because we keep His commandments and do those things that are pleasing in His sight.

1 JOHN 5:14-15 (NLT)
14 And we are confident that he hears us whenever we ask for anything that pleases him.
15 And since we know he hears us when we make our requests, we also know that he will give us what we ask for.

3 JOHN 2 (NKJV) Beloved, I pray that you may prosper in all things and be in health, just as your soul prospers.

REVELATION 12:11 (NKJV) And they overcame him by the blood of the Lamb and by the word of their testimony, and they did not love their lives to the death.

Identity, Confidence, Insecurity

⤜⋆⤛

GENESIS 1:27-28 (NIV)
27 So God created mankind in his own image, in the image of God he created them; male and female he created them.
28 God blessed them and said to them, "Be fruitful and increase in number; fill the earth and subdue it. Rule over the fish in the sea and the birds in the sky and over every living creature that moves on the ground."

DEUTERONOMY 28:13 (NLT) If you listen to these commands of the LORD your God that I am giving you today, and if you carefully obey them, the LORD will make you the head and not the tail, and you will always be on top and never at the bottom.

PSALM 139:13-14 (TPT)
13 You formed my innermost being, shaping my delicate inside and my intricate outside, and wove them all together in my mother's womb.

The Pocket Prayer

14 I thank you, God, for making me so mysteriously complex! Everything you do is marvelously breathtaking. It simply amazes me to think about it! How thoroughly you know me, Lord!

ISAIAH 49:16 (NKJV) See, I have inscribed you on the palms of My hands; Your walls are continually before Me.

JEREMIAH 29:11 (NIV) "For I know the plans I have for you," declares the LORD, "plans to prosper you and not to harm you, plans to give you hope and a future."

LUKE 11:9-10 (NLT)
9 And so I tell you, keep on asking, and you will receive what you ask for. Keep on seeking, and you will find. Keep on knocking, and the door will be opened to you.
10 For everyone who asks, receives. Everyone who seeks, finds. And to everyone who knocks, the door will be opened.

JOHN 15:16 (NKJV) You did not choose Me, but I chose you and appointed you that you should go and bear fruit, and that your fruit should remain, that whatever you ask the Father in My name He may give you.

PHILIPPIANS 1:6 (TLB) And I am sure that God who began the good work within you will keep right on helping you grow in his grace until his task within you is finally finished on that day when Jesus Christ returns.

ROMANS 8:14 (TLB) For all who are led by the Spirit of God are sons of God.

EPHESIANS 2:10 (ESV) For we are his workmanship, created in Christ Jesus for good works, which God prepared beforehand, that we should walk in them.

COLOSSIANS 2:10 (NLT) So you also are complete through your union with Christ, who is the head over every ruler and authority.

2 TIMOTHY 1:7 (NKJV) For God has not given us a spirit of fear, but of power and of love and of a sound mind.

The Pocket Prayer

1 JOHN 3:1 (NLT) See how very much our Father loves us, for he calls us his children, and that is what we are! But the people who belong to this world don't recognize that we are God's children because they don't know him.

GALATIANS 4:7 (NLT) Now you are no longer a slave but God's own child. And since you are his child, God has made you his heir.

2 CORINTHIANS 5:20-21 (NIV)
20 We are therefore Christ's ambassadors, as though God were making his appeal through us. We implore you on Christ's behalf: Be reconciled to God.
21 God made him who had no sin to be sin for us, so that in him we might become the righteousness of God.

1 PETER 2:9 (NIV) But you are a chosen people, a royal priesthood, a holy nation, God's special possession, that you may declare the praises of him who called you out of darkness into his wonderful light.

EPHESIANS 2:19 (NLT) So now you Gentiles are no longer strangers and foreigners. You are citizens along with all of God's holy people. You are members of God's family.

PHILIPPIANS 1:6 (NKJV) Being confident of this very thing, that He who has begun a good work in you will complete it until the day of Jesus Christ;

EPHESIANS 1:11 (ESV) In him we have obtained an inheritance, having been predestined according to the purpose of him who works all things according to the counsel of his will,

2 CORINTHIANS 5:7 (NKJV) For we walk by faith, not by sight.

ROMANS 8:16-17 (NKJV)
16 The Spirit Himself bears witness with our spirit that we are children of God,
17 and if children, then heirs—heirs of God and joint heirs with Christ, if indeed we suffer with Him, that we may also be glorified together.

ROMANS 8:37 (NLT) No, despite all these things, overwhelming victory is ours through Christ, who loved us.

The Pocket Prayer

ACTS 1:8 (NLT) But you will receive power when the Holy Spirit comes upon you. And you will be my witnesses, telling people about me everywhere—in Jerusalem, throughout Judea, in Samaria, and to the ends of the earth.

EPHESIANS 1:19-21 (NLT)
19 I also pray that you will understand the incredible greatness of God's power for us who believe him. This is the same mighty power
20 that raised Christ from the dead and seated him in the place of honor at God's right hand in the heavenly realms.
21 Now he is far above any ruler or authority or power or leader or anything else—not only in this world but also in the world to come.

EPHESIANS 2:6-7 (NASB)
6 and raised us up with Him, and seated us with Him in the heavenly places in Christ Jesus,
7 so that in the ages to come He might show the surpassing riches of His grace in kindness toward us in Christ Jesus.

2 CORINTHIANS 12:9 (NASB) And He has said to me, "My grace is sufficient for you, for power is perfected in weakness." Most gladly, therefore, I will rather boast about my weaknesses, so that the power of Christ may dwell in me.

ISAIAH 54:17 (NIV) No weapon forged against you will prevail, and you will refute every tongue that accuses you. This is the heritage of the servants of the LORD, and this is their vindication from me," declares the LORD.

MATTHEW 5:13-14 (NIV)
13 "You are the salt of the earth. But if the salt loses its saltiness, how can it be made salty again? It is no longer good for anything, except to be thrown out and trampled underfoot.
14 "You are the light of the world. A town built on a hill cannot be hidden.

Joy

∽

ISAIAH 12:3 (TLB) Oh, the joy of drinking deeply from the Fountain of Salvation!

ISAIAH 12:5-6 (NASB)
5 Praise the Lord in song, for He has done excellent things; Let this be known throughout the earth.
6 Cry aloud and shout for joy, O inhabitants of Zion, For great in your midst is the Holy One of Israel.

ROMANS 15:13 (NIV) May the God of hope fill you with all joy and peace as you trust in him, so that you may overflow with hope by the power of the Holy Spirit.

ROMANS 14:17 (NASB) For the kingdom of God is not eating and drinking, but righteousness and peace and joy in the Holy Spirit.

GALATIANS 5:22-23 (NLT)
22 But the Holy Spirit produces this kind of fruit in our lives: love, joy,

peace, patience, kindness, goodness, faithfulness,
23 gentleness, and self-control. There is no law against these things!

PROVERBS 17:22 (NLT) A cheerful heart is good medicine, but a broken spirit saps a person's strength.

PROVERBS 15:15 (AMP) All the days of the afflicted are bad, But a glad heart has a continual feast [regardless of the circumstances].

PROVERBS 15:23 (NLV) To give a good answer is a joy to a man, and how pleasing is a word given at the right time!

PSALM 5:11 (NLV) But let all who put their trust in You be glad. Let them sing with joy forever. You make a covering for them, that all who love Your name may be glad in You.

PSALM 32:11 (TPT) So celebrate the goodness of God! He shows this kindness to everyone who is his. Go ahead—shout for joy, all you upright ones who want to please him!

The Pocket Prayer

PSALM 68:3 (NLT) But let the godly rejoice. Let them be glad in God's presence. Let them be filled with joy.

PSALM 4:7 (NLT) You have given me greater joy than those who have abundant harvests of grain and new wine.

PHILIPPIANS 1:25 (NLT) Knowing this, I am convinced that I will remain alive so I can continue to help all of you grow and experience the joy of your faith.

PHILIPPIANS 4:4 (NKJV) Rejoice in the Lord always. Again I will say, rejoice!

1 PETER 1:8 (NIV) Though you have not seen him, you love him; and even though you do not see him now, you believe in him and are filled with an inexpressible and glorious joy,

JOB 5:21-22 (NLT)
21 You will be safe from slander and have no fear when destruction comes.
22 You will laugh at destruction and famine wild animals will not terrify you.

Pamela Christian Flickinger

PSALM 2:4 (NLT) But the one who rules in heaven laughs. The Lord scoffs at them.

JEREMIAH 15:16 (NLT) When I discovered your words, I devoured them. They are my joy and my heart's delight, for I bear your name, O LORD God of Heaven's Armies.

PSALM 119:162 (NLT) I rejoice in your word like one who discovers a great treasure.

NEHEMIAH 8:10 (NIV) Nehemiah said, "Go and enjoy choice food and sweet drinks, and send some to those who have nothing prepared. This day is holy to our Lord. Do not grieve, for the joy of the LORD is your strength."

JOB 8:21 (TLB) He will yet fill your mouth with laughter and your lips with shouts of joy.

JOHN 16:24 (ESV) Until now you have asked nothing in my name. Ask, and you will receive, that your joy may be full.

The Pocket Prayer

PSALM 89:15-16 (HCSB)
15 Happy are the people who know the joyful shout; Yahweh, they walk in the light of Your presence.
16 They rejoice in Your name all day long, and they are exalted by Your righteousness.

HEBREWS 1:9 (NLT) You love justice and hate evil. Therefore, O God, your God has anointed you, pouring out the oil of joy on you more than on anyone else.

HABAKKUK 3:17-19 (NLT)
17 Even though the fig trees have no blossoms, and there are no grapes on the vines; even though the olive crop fails, and the fields lie empty and barren; even though the flocks die in the fields, and the cattle barns are empty,
18 yet I will rejoice in the LORD! I will be joyful in the God of my salvation!
19 The Sovereign LORD is my strength! He makes me as surefooted as a deer, able to tread upon the heights.

JAMES 1:2-3 (NLT)
2 Dear brothers and sisters, when troubles

of any kind come your way, consider it an opportunity for great joy.
3 For you know that when your faith is tested, your endurance has a chance to grow.

ISAIAH 55:12 (NIV) You will go out in joy and be led forth in peace; the mountains and hills will burst into song before you, and all the trees of the field will clap their hands.

ISAIAH 66:14 (AMP) When you see this, your heart will rejoice; Your bones will flourish like new grass. And the [powerful] hand of the LORD will be revealed to His servants, But His indignation will be toward His enemies.

Love

∽

JOHN 14:23 (NLT) Jesus replied, "All who love me will do what I say. My Father will love them, and we will come and make our home with each of them.

JOHN 3:16-17 (TLB)
16 For God loved the world so much that he gave his only Son so that anyone who believes in him shall not perish but have eternal life.
17 God did not send his Son into the world to condemn it, but to save it.

1 JOHN 4:17-19 (NIV)
17 This is how love is made complete among us so that we will have confidence on the day of judgment: In this world we are like Jesus.
18 There is no fear in love. But perfect love drives out fear, because fear has to do with punishment. The one who fears is not made perfect in love.
19 We love because he first loved us.

1 JOHN 4:7-8 (NLT)
7 Dear friends, let us continue to love one another, for love comes from God. Anyone who loves is a child of God and knows God.
8 But anyone who does not love does not know God, for God is love.

1 JOHN 4:11 (NLT) Dear friends, since God loved us that much, we surely ought to love each other.

COLOSSIANS 3:14 (ESV) And above all these put on love, which binds everything together in perfect harmony.

MARK 12:33 (HCSB) And to love Him with all your heart, with all your understanding, and with all your strength, and to love your neighbor as yourself, is far more important than all the burnt offerings and sacrifices.

MATTHEW 5:44 (ESV) But I say to you, Love your enemies and pray for those who persecute you,

DEUTERONOMY 30:6 (NLT) The LORD your God will change your heart and the hearts of all your descendants, so

The Pocket Prayer

that you will love him with all your heart and soul and so you may live!

2 JOHN 6 (NLT) Love means doing what God has commanded us, and he has commanded us to love one another, just as you heard from the beginning.

JOHN 13:34-35 (NLT)
34 So now I am giving you a new commandment: Love each other. Just as I have loved you, you should love each other.
35 Your love for one another will prove to the world that you are my disciples.

HEBREWS 12:6 (NLT) For the Lord disciplines those he loves, and he punishes each one he accepts as his child.

JOHN 15:10 (NIV) If you keep my commands, you will remain in my love, just as I have kept my Father's commands and remain in his love.

ROMANS 5:5 (NASB) And hope does not disappoint, because the love of God has been poured out within our hearts through the Holy Spirit who was given to us.

EPHESIANS 5:1 (NKJV) Therefore be imitators of God as dear children.

1 CORINTHIANS 13:4-7 (NIV)
4 Love is patient, love is kind. It does not envy, it does not boast, it is not proud.
5 It does not dishonor others, it is not self-seeking, it is not easily angered, it keeps no record of wrongs.
6 Love does not delight in evil but rejoices with the truth.
7 It always protects, always trusts, always hopes, always perseveres.

GALATIANS 5:6 (NLT) For when we place our faith in Christ Jesus, there is no benefit in being circumcised or being uncircumcised. What is important is faith expressing itself in love.

PSALM 32:10 (NLT) Many sorrows come to the wicked, but unfailing love surrounds those who trust the LORD.

EPHESIANS 4:15 (NLT) Instead, we will speak the truth in love, growing in every way more and more like Christ, who is the head of his body, the church.

The Pocket Prayer

1 PETER 3:8 (NLT) Finally, all of you should be of one mind. Sympathize with each other. Love each other as brothers and sisters. Be tenderhearted, and keep a humble attitude.

GALATIANS 5:22 (NLT) But the Holy Spirit produces this kind of fruit in our lives: love, joy, peace, patience, kindness, goodness, faithfulness,

1 CORINTHIANS 16:14 (NLT) And do everything with love.

1 PETER 4:8 (NLT) Most important of all, continue to show deep love for each other, for love covers a multitude of sins.

ROMANS 13:10 (NLT) Love does no wrong to others, so love fulfills the requirements of God's law.

EPHESIANS 3:17-19 (NIV)
17 so that Christ may dwell in your hearts through faith. And I pray that you, being rooted and established in love,
18 may have power, together with all the Lord's holy people, to grasp how wide and long and high and deep is the love of Christ,

19 and to know this love that surpasses knowledge—that you may be filled to the measure of all the fullness of God.

EPHESIANS 4:1-3 (ESV)
1 I therefore, a prisoner for the Lord, urge you to walk in a manner worthy of the calling to which you have been called,
2 with all humility and gentleness, with patience, bearing with one another in love,
3 eager to maintain the unity of the Spirit in the bond of peace.

ROMANS 12:9-10 (HCSB)
9 Love must be without hypocrisy. Detest evil; cling to what is good.
10 Show family affection to one another with brotherly love. Outdo one another in showing honor.

1 CHRONICLES 16:34 (NLT) Give thanks to the Lord, for he is good! His faithful love endures forever.

1 JOHN 3:18 (TLB) Little children, let us stop just saying we love people; let us really love them, and show it by our actions.

The Pocket Prayer

1 THESSALONIANS 3:12 (NIV) May the Lord make your love increase and overflow for each other and for everyone else, just as ours does for you.

EPHESIANS 4:31-32 (NIV)
31 Get rid of all bitterness, rage and anger, brawling and slander, along with every form of malice.
32 Be kind and compassionate to one another, forgiving each other, just as in Christ God forgave you.

Peace

❦

ISAIAH 26:3 (TLB) He will keep in perfect peace all those who trust in him, whose thoughts turn often to the Lord!

2 TIMOTHY 1:7 (NKJV) For God has not given us a spirit of fear, but of power and of love and of a sound mind.

ISAIAH 54:14-15 (NIV)
14 In righteousness you will be established: Tyranny will be far from you; you will have nothing to fear. Terror will be far removed; it will not come near you.
15 If anyone does attack you, it will not be my doing; whoever attacks you will surrender to you.

PSALM 4:8 (NLT) In peace I will lie down and sleep, for you alone, O Lord, will keep me safe.

PHILIPPIANS 4:6-7 (NLT)
6 Don't worry about anything; instead, pray about everything. Tell God what you need, and thank him for all he has done.
7 Then you will experience God's

The Pocket Prayer

peace, which exceeds anything we can understand. His peace will guard your hearts and minds as you live in Christ Jesus.

1 PETER 5:7 (NLT) Give all your worries and cares to God, for he cares about you.

LUKE 10:19 (NKJV) Behold, I give you the authority to trample on serpents and scorpions, and over all the power of the enemy, and nothing shall by any means hurt you.

PSALM 55:16-17 (NLT)
16 But I will call on God, and the Lord will rescue me.
17 Morning, noon, and night I cry out in my distress, and the Lord hears my voice.

GENESIS 28:15 (NIV) I am with you and will watch over you wherever you go, and I will bring you back to this land. I will not leave you until I have done what I have promised you.

JOSHUA 1:9 (NKJV) Have I not commanded you? Be strong and of good courage; do not be afraid, nor be dismayed, for the Lord your God is with you wherever you go.

PROVERBS 3:24 (NKJV) When you lie down, you will not be afraid; Yes, you will lie down and your sleep will be sweet.

MATTHEW 6:25 (NLT) That is why I tell you not to worry about everyday life—whether you have enough food and drink, or enough clothes to wear. Isn't life more than food, and your body more than clothing?

1 JOHN 4:18 (NLT) Such love has no fear, because perfect love expels all fear. If we are afraid, it is for fear of punishment, and this shows that we have not fully experienced his perfect love.

2 CORINTHIANS 10:5 (NASB) We are destroying speculations and every lofty thing raised up against the knowledge of God, and we are taking every thought captive to the obedience of Christ,

PSALM 119:165 (TLB) Those who love your laws have great peace of heart and mind and do not stumble.

The Pocket Prayer

JOHN 14:27 (ESV) Peace I leave with you; my peace I give to you. Not as the world gives do I give to you. Let not your hearts be troubled, neither let them be afraid.

HAGGAI 2:9 (NIV) 'The glory of this present house will be greater than the glory of the former house,' says the LORD Almighty. 'And in this place I will grant peace,' declares the LORD Almighty."

ISAIAH 57:19 (NKJV) "I create the fruit of the lips: Peace, peace to him who is far off and to him who is near," Says the Lord, "And I will heal him."

COLOSSIANS 3:15 (NASB) Let the peace of Christ [a]rule in your hearts, to which indeed you were called in one body; and be thankful.

JOHN 16:33 (NLT) I have told you all this so that you may have peace in me. Here on earth you will have many trials and sorrows. But take heart, because I have overcome the world.

HEBREWS 12:14 (NLT) Work at living in peace with everyone, and work at living a holy life, for those who are not holy will not see the Lord.

PHILIPPIANS 4:8 (NIV) Finally, brothers and sisters, whatever is true, whatever is noble, whatever is right, whatever is pure, whatever is lovely, whatever is admirable—if anything is excellent or praiseworthy—think about such things.

NUMBERS 6:24-26 (NLT)
24 May the Lord bless you and protect you.
25 May the Lord smile on you
and be gracious to you.
26 May the Lord show you his favor and give you his peace.

MATTHEW 11:28-29 (NIV)
28 Come to me, all you who are weary and burdened, and I will give you rest.
29 Take my yoke upon you and learn from me, for I am gentle and humble in heart, and you will find rest for your souls.

PSALM 29:11 (TLB) He will give his people strength. He will bless them with peace.

The Pocket Prayer

PHILIPPIANS 4:9 (NKJV) The things which you learned and received and heard and saw in me, these do, and the God of peace will be with you.

PSALM 121:2-8 (NLT)
2 My help comes from the LORD, who made heaven and earth!
3 He will not let you stumble; the one who watches over you will not slumber.
4 Indeed, he who watches over Israel never slumbers or sleeps.
5 The LORD himself watches over you! The LORD stands beside you as your protective shade.
6 The sun will not harm you by day, nor the moon at night.
7 The LORD keeps you from all harm and watches over your life.
8 The LORD keeps watch over you as you come and go, both now and forever.

Protection

❦

JOB 1:10 (NLT) You have always put a wall of protection around him and his home and his property. You have made him prosper in everything he does. Look how rich he is!

GENESIS 15:1 (NIV) After this, the word of the LORD came to Abram in a vision: "Do not be afraid, Abram. I am your shield, your very great reward."

DEUTERONOMY 33:27-29 (NLT)
27 The eternal God is your refuge, and his everlasting arms are under you. He drives out the enemy before you; he cries out, 'Destroy them!'
28 So Israel will live in safety, prosperous Jacob in security, in a land of grain and new wine, while the heavens drop down dew.
29 How blessed you are, O Israel! Who else is like you, a people saved by the LORD? He is your protecting shield and your triumphant sword! Your enemies

The Pocket Prayer

will cringe before you, and you will stomp on their backs!"

2 SAMUEL 22:2-4 (NLT)
2 He sang: "The LORD is my rock, my fortress, and my savior;
3 My God is my rock, in whom I find protection. He is my shield, the power that saves me, and my place of safety. He is my refuge, my savior, the one who saves me from violence.
4 I called on the LORD, who is worthy of praise, and he saved me from my enemies.

PSALM 3:6-7 (NKJV)
6 I will not be afraid of ten thousands of people Who have set themselves against me all around.
7 Arise, O Lord; Save me, O my God! For You have struck all my enemies on the cheekbone; You have broken the teeth of the ungodly.

1 JOHN 5:4 (NLT) For every child of God defeats this evil world, and we achieve this victory through our faith.

PSALM 9:9 (NLT) The LORD is a shelter for the oppressed, a refuge in times of trouble.

PSALM 18:29 (NLT) In your strength I can crush an army; with my God I can scale any wall.

PSALM 27:2 (NLT) When evil people come to devour me, when my enemies and foes attack me, they will stumble and fall.

PSALM 27:5 (NLT) For he will conceal me there when troubles come; he will hide me in his sanctuary. He will place me out of reach on a high rock.

PSALM 56:4 (NLT) I praise God for what he has promised. I trust in God, so why should I be afraid? What can mere mortals do to me?

PSALM 91:5-7 (NLT)
5 Do not be afraid of the terrors of the night, nor the arrow that flies in the day.
6 Do not dread the disease that stalks in darkness, nor the disaster that strikes at midday.
7 Though a thousand fall at your side,

The Pocket Prayer

though ten thousand are dying around you, these evils will not touch you.

PSALM 91:9-11 (NLT)
9 If you make the LORD your refuge, if you make the Most High your shelter,
10 no evil will conquer you; no plague will come near your home.
11 For he will order his angels to protect you wherever you go.

ISAIAH 43:1-2 (NLT)
1 But now, O Jacob, listen to the LORD who created you. O Israel, the one who formed you says, "Do not be afraid, for I have ransomed you. I have called you by name; you are mine.
2 When you go through deep waters, I will be with you. When you go through rivers of difficulty, you will not drown. When you walk through the fire of oppression, you will not be burned up; the flames will not consume you.

MATTHEW 6:13 (NIV) And lead us not into temptation, but deliver us from the evil one.

MARK 16:18 (NLT) They will be able to handle snakes with safety, and if they drink anything poisonous, it won't hurt them. They will be able to place their hands on the sick, and they will be healed.

PROVERBS 18:10 (NLT) The name of the LORD is a strong fortress; the godly run to him and are safe.

PROVERBS 30:5 (NLT) Every word of God proves true. He is a shield to all who come to him for protection.

ISAIAH 54:17 (NIV) "No weapon forged against you will prevail, and you will refute every tongue that accuses you. This is the heritage of the servants of the LORD, and this is their vindication from me," declares the LORD.

LUKE 10:19 (NIV) I have given you authority to trample on snakes and scorpions and to overcome all the power of the enemy; nothing will harm you.

EPHESIANS 6:11 (TPT) Put on God's complete set of armor provided for us, so that you will be protected as you fight against the evil strategies of the accuser!

The Pocket Prayer

PSALM 4:8 (NLT) In peace I will lie down and sleep, for you alone, O LORD, will keep me safe.

PSALM 27:1 (NLT) The LORD is my light and my salvation— so why should I be afraid? The LORD is my fortress, protecting me from danger, so why should I tremble?

PSALM 121:2-8 (NLT)
2 My help comes from the LORD, who made heaven and earth!
3 He will not let you stumble; the one who watches over you will not slumber.
4 Indeed, he who watches over Israel never slumbers or sleeps.
5 The LORD himself watches over you! The LORD stands beside you as your protective shade.
6 The sun will not harm you by day, nor the moon at night.
7 The LORD keeps you from all harm and watches over your life.
8 The LORD keeps watch over you as you come and go, both now and forever.

Pamela Christian Flickinger

PSALM 145:19-20 (NLT)
19 He grants the desires of those who fear him; he hears their cries for help and rescues them.
20 The LORD protects all those who love him, but he destroys the wicked.

PROVERBS 3:24-26 (NLT)
24 You can go to bed without fear; you will lie down and sleep soundly.
25 You need not be afraid of sudden disaster or the destruction that comes upon the wicked,
26 for the LORD is your security. He will keep your foot from being caught in a trap.

JOSHUA 1:5 (NLT) No one will be able to stand against you as long as you live. For I will be with you as I was with Moses. I will not fail you or abandon you.

PSALM 5:11 (NLT) But let all who take refuge in you rejoice; let them sing joyful praises forever. Spread your protection over them, that all who love your name may be filled with joy.

PSALM 31:4 (NLT) Pull me from the trap my enemies set for me, for I find protection in you alone.

PSALM 34:7 (NLT) For the angel of the LORD is a guard; he surrounds and defends all who fear him.

PSALM 34:20 (NLT) For the LORD protects the bones of the righteous; not one of them is broken!

Salvation

JOHN 3:16 (NIV) For God so loved the world that he gave his one and only Son, that whoever believes in him shall not perish but have eternal life.

DEUTERONOMY 31:6 (NKJV) Be strong and of good courage, do not fear nor be afraid of them; for the Lord your God, He is the One who goes with you. He will not leave you nor forsake you.

GALATIANS 3:13-14 (NLT)
13 But Christ has rescued us from the curse pronounced by the law. When he was hung on the cross, he took upon himself the curse for our wrongdoing. For it is written in the Scriptures, "Cursed is everyone who is hung on a tree."
14 Through Christ Jesus, God has blessed the Gentiles with the same blessing he promised to Abraham, so that we who are believers might receive the promised Holy Spirit through faith.

The Pocket Prayer

JAMES 1:22 (NLT) But don't just listen to God's word. You must do what it says. Otherwise, you are only fooling yourselves.

ACTS 2:21 (NLT) But everyone who calls on the name of the LORD will be saved.

ROMANS 8:16 (TLB) For his Holy Spirit speaks to us deep in our hearts and tells us that we really are God's children.

EZEKIEL 36:26-27 (NIV)
26 I will give you a new heart and put a new spirit in you; I will remove from you your heart of stone and give you a heart of flesh.
27 And I will put my Spirit in you and move you to follow my decrees and be careful to keep my laws.

ROMANS 6:23 (NLT) For the wages of sin is death, but the free gift of God is eternal life through Christ Jesus our Lord.

1 JOHN 5:10 (NLT) All who believe in the Son of God know in their hearts that this testimony is true. Those who don't believe this are actually calling God a liar

because they don't believe what God has testified about his Son.

JOHN 3:3 (NLT) Jesus replied, "I tell you the truth, unless you are born again, you cannot see the Kingdom of God."

EPHESIANS 2:8 (NLT) God saved you by his grace when you believed. And you can't take credit for this; it is a gift from God.

PSALM 27:1 (NLT) The LORD is my light and my salvation— so why should I be afraid? The LORD is my fortress, protecting me from danger, so why should I tremble?

1 JOHN 1:9 (NLT) But if we confess our sins to him, he is faithful and just to forgive us our sins and to cleanse us from all wickedness.

3 JOHN 4 (NLT) I could have no greater joy than to hear that my children are following the truth.

2 TIMOTHY 2:21 (NLT) If you keep yourself pure, you will be a special utensil for honorable use. Your life will be clean,

The Pocket Prayer

and you will be ready for the Master to use you for every good work.

2 TIMOTHY 2:25-26 (NLT)
25 Gently instruct those who oppose the truth. Perhaps God will change those people's hearts, and they will learn the truth.
26 Then they will come to their senses and escape from the devil's trap. For they have been held captive by him to do whatever he wants.

JOHN 8:24 (NLT) That is why I said that you will die in your sins; for unless you believe that I AM who I claim to be, you will die in your sins.

JAMES 4:8 (NLT) Come close to God, and God will come close to you. Wash your hands, you sinners; purify your hearts, for your loyalty is divided between God and the world.

2 CORINTHIANS 5:17 (NIV) Therefore, if anyone is in Christ, the new creation has come: The old has gone, the new is here!

ROMANS 6:11 (HCSB) So, you too consider yourselves dead to sin but alive to God in Christ Jesus.

2 CORINTHIANS 5:20-21 (NIV)
20 We are therefore Christ's ambassadors, as though God were making his appeal through us. We implore you on Christ's behalf: Be reconciled to God.
21 God made him who had no sin to be sin for us, so that in him we might become the righteousness of God.

GALATIANS 2:20 (ESV) I have been crucified with Christ. It is no longer I who live, but Christ who lives in me. And the life I now live in the flesh I live by faith in the Son of God, who loved me and gave himself for me.

ROMANS 5:8-9 (NKJV)
8 But God demonstrates His own love toward us, in that while we were still sinners, Christ died for us.
9 Much more then, having now been justified by His blood, we shall be saved from wrath through Him.

The Pocket Prayer

2 CORINTHIANS 6:2 (ESV) For he says, "In a favorable time I listened to you, and in a day of salvation I have helped you." Behold, now is the favorable time; behold, now is the day of salvation.

ROMANS 3:23-24 (NLT)
23 For everyone has sinned; we all fall short of God's glorious standard.
24 Yet God, in his grace, freely makes us right in his sight. He did this through Christ Jesus when he freed us from the penalty for our sins.

ROMANS 10:9-10 (NLT)
9 If you openly declare that Jesus is Lord and believe in your heart that God raised him from the dead, you will be saved.
10 For it is by believing in your heart that you are made right with God, and it is by openly declaring your faith that you are saved.

MATTHEW 10:32 (NLT) Everyone who acknowledges me publicly here on earth, I will also acknowledge before my Father in heaven.

PHILIPPIANS 4:13 (NLT) For I can do everything through Christ, who gives me strength.

COLOSSIANS 1:13-14 (NLT)
13 For he has rescued us from the kingdom of darkness and transferred us into the Kingdom of his dear Son,
14 who purchased our freedom and forgave our sins.

Strength

∽

PHILIPPIANS 4:13 (NLT) For I can do everything through Christ, who gives me strength.

MARK 14:38 (ESV) Watch and pray that you may not enter into temptation. The spirit indeed is willing, but the flesh is weak.

JOEL 3:9-10 (NIV)
9 Proclaim this among the nations: Prepare for war! Rouse the warriors! Let all the fighting men draw near and attack. 10 Beat your plowshares into swords and your pruning hooks into spears. Let the weakling say, "I am strong!"

ZECHARIAH 4:6 (TLB) Then he said, "This is God's message to Zerubbabel: 'Not by might, nor by power, but by my Spirit, says the Lord Almighty—you will succeed because of my Spirit, though you are few and weak.'"

ISAIAH 40:31 (NKJV) But those who wait on the Lord Shall renew their strength; They shall mount up with wings like eagles, They shall run and not be weary, They shall walk and not faint.

ISAIAH 41:10 (TLB) Fear not, for I am with you. Do not be dismayed. I am your God. I will strengthen you; I will help you; I will uphold you with my victorious right hand.

JOHN 16:33 (NLT) I have told you all this so that you may have peace in me. Here on earth you will have many trials and sorrows. But take heart, because I have overcome the world.

ROMANS 8:37 (NLT) No, despite all these things, overwhelming victory is ours through Christ, who loved us.

2 CORINTHIANS 5:7 (NKJV) For we walk by faith, not by sight.

PSALM 18:29 (NLT) In your strength I can crush an army; with my God I can scale any wall.

PSALM 18:35 (NLT) You have given me your shield of victory. Your right hand

The Pocket Prayer

supports me; your help has made me great.

2 CORINTHIANS 1:21 (ESV) And it is God who establishes us with you in Christ, and has anointed us,

HEBREWS 4:16 (HCSB) Therefore let us approach the throne of grace with boldness, so that we may receive mercy and find grace to help us at the proper time.

ACTS 1:8 (NLT) But you will receive power when the Holy Spirit comes upon you. And you will be my witnesses, telling people about me everywhere—in Jerusalem, throughout Judea, Samaria, and to the ends of the earth.

2 SAMUEL 22:34 (NLT) He makes me as surefooted as a deer, enabling me to stand on mountain heights.

PROVERBS 14:26 (NLT) Those who fear the LORD are secure; he will be a refuge for their children.

1 SAMUEL 2:4 (NLT) The bow of the mighty is now broken, and those who stumbled are now strong.

2 SAMUEL 22:3 (NLT) My God is my rock, in whom I find protection. He is my shield, the power that saves me, and my place of safety. He is my refuge, my savior, the one who saves me from violence.

PSALM 28:7 (NLT) The LORD is my strength and shield. I trust him with all my heart. He helps me, and my heart is filled with joy. I burst out in songs of thanksgiving.

PSALM 29:11 (NLT) The LORD gives his people strength. The LORD blesses them with peace.

2 PETER 1:3 (NIV) His divine power has given us everything we need for a godly life through our knowledge of him who called us by his own glory and goodness.

ISAIAH 40:29-30 (NIV)
29 He gives strength to the weary and increases the power of the weak.

The Pocket Prayer

30 Even youths grow tired and weary, and young men stumble and fall;

2 CORINTHIANS 12:10 (NIV) That is why, for Christ's sake, I delight in weaknesses, in insults, in hardships, in persecutions, in difficulties. For when I am weak, then I am strong.

JUDE 24-25 (NLT)
24 Now all glory to God, who is able to keep you from falling away and will bring you with great joy into his glorious presence without a single fault.
25 All glory to him who alone is God, our Savior through Jesus Christ our Lord. All glory, majesty, power, and authority are his before all time, and in the present, and beyond all time! Amen.

PSALM 59:17 (NLT) O my Strength, to you I sing praises, for you, O God, are my refuge, the God who shows me unfailing love.

PSALM 62:11 (NLT) God has spoken plainly, and I have heard it many times: Power, O God, belongs to you;

Wisdom, Understanding

※

1 CORINTHIANS 1:30 (NLT) God has united you with Christ Jesus. For our benefit God made him to be wisdom itself. Christ made us right with God; he made us pure and holy, and he freed us from sin.

EPHESIANS 1:17-18 (NIV)
17 I keep asking that the God of our Lord Jesus Christ, the glorious Father, may give you the Spirit of wisdom and revelation, so that you may know him better.
18 I pray that the eyes of your heart may be enlightened in order that you may know the hope to which he has called you, the riches of his glorious inheritance in his holy people,

DEUTERONOMY 29:29 (NLT) The Lord our God has secrets known to no one. We are not accountable for them, but we and our children are accountable forever for all that he has revealed to us, so that we may obey all the terms of these instructions.

The Pocket Prayer

PSALM 49:3 (NKJV) My mouth shall speak wisdom, And the meditation of my heart shall give understanding.

PSALM 51:6 (NIV) I know that you delight to set your truth deep in my spirit. So come into the hidden places of my heart and teach me wisdom.

ECCLESIASTES 7:12 (NLT) Wisdom and money can get you almost anything, but only wisdom can save your life.

PROVERBS 1:5 (NLT) Let the wise listen to these proverbs and become even wiser. Let those with understanding receive guidance

PROVERBS 2:10-11 (NLT)
10 For wisdom will enter your heart, and knowledge will fill you with joy.
11 Wise choices will watch over you. Understanding will keep you safe.

PROVERBS 4:5-7 (NLT)
5 Get wisdom; develop good judgment. Don't forget my words or turn away from them.
6 Don't turn your back on wisdom, for

she will protect you. Love her, and she will guard you.

7 Getting wisdom is the wisest thing you can do! And whatever else you do, develop good judgment.

PROVERBS 8:12-14 (NLT)
12 "I, Wisdom, live together with good judgment. I know where to discover knowledge and discernment.
13 All who fear the LORD will hate evil. Therefore, I hate pride and arrogance, corruption and perverse speech.
14 Common sense and success belong to me. Insight and strength are mine."

PROVERBS 13:20 (NLT) Walk with the wise and become wise; associate with fools and get in trouble.

PROVERBS 28:26 (NLT) Those who trust their own insight are foolish, but anyone who walks in wisdom is safe.

LUKE 21:15 (NLT) For I will give you the right words and such wisdom that none of your opponents will be able to reply or refute you!

The Pocket Prayer

1 CORINTHIANS 2:16 (NLT) For, "Who can know the LORD's thoughts? Who knows enough to teach him?" But we understand these things, for we have the mind of Christ.

JAMES 1:5 (NIV) If any of you lacks wisdom, you should ask God, who gives generously to all without finding fault, and it will be given to you.

PROVERBS 3:35 (NASB) The wise will inherit honor, But fools display dishonor.

ISAIAH 28:29 (ESV) This also comes from the Lord of hosts; he is wonderful in counsel and excellent in wisdom.

PROVERBS 2:12 (NLT) Wisdom will save you from evil people, from those whose words are twisted.

PSALM 119:103-104 (NIV)
103 How sweet are your words to my taste, sweeter than honey to my mouth!
104 I gain understanding from your precepts; therefore I hate every wrong path.

MATTHEW 13:12 (NLT) To those who listen to my teaching, more understanding will be given, and they will have an abundance of knowledge. But for those who are not listening, even what little understanding they have will be taken away from them.

LUKE 8:18 (NLT) "So pay attention to how you hear. To those who listen to my teaching, more understanding will be given. But for those who are not listening, even what they think they understand will be taken away from them."

1 CORINTHIANS 2:12 (NIV) What we have received is not the spirit of the world, but the Spirit who is from God, so that we may understand what God has freely given us.

JOB 12:13-14 (NLT)
13 But true wisdom and power are found in God; counsel and understanding are his.
14 What he destroys cannot be rebuilt. When he puts someone in prison, there is no escape.

The Pocket Prayer

JOB 28:28 (NLT) And this is what he says to all humanity: "The fear of the Lord is true wisdom; to forsake evil is real understanding."

PSALM 19:7 (NLT) The instructions of the LORD are perfect, reviving the soul. The decrees of the LORD are trustworthy, making wise the simple.

PROVERBS 2:6-7 (NLT)
6 For the LORD grants wisdom! From his mouth come knowledge and understanding.
7 He grants a treasure of common sense to the honest. He is a shield to those who walk with integrity.

PROVERBS 4:8 (NLT) If you prize wisdom, she will make you great. Embrace her, and she will honor you.

Prayer of Salvation

Heavenly Father, I come to You in the Name of Jesus. Your Word says, "Whosoever shall call on the name of the Lord shall be saved" (Acts 2:21). I am calling on You. I pray and ask Jesus to come into my heart and be Lord over my life according to Romans 10:9-10 (NIV): *"If you declare with your mouth, "Jesus is Lord," and believe in your heart that God raised him from the dead, you will be saved. For it is with your heart that you believe and are justified, and it is with your mouth that you profess your faith and are saved."* I do that now.

I confess that Jesus is Lord, and I believe in my heart that God raised Him from the dead. I am now reborn! I am a Christian—a child of Almighty God! I am saved!

You also said in Your Word, *"If ye then, being evil, know how to give good gifts unto your children: HOW MUCH MORE shall your heavenly Father give*

Pamela Christian Flickinger

the Holy Spirit to them that ask him?" (Luke 11:13). I'm also asking You to fill me with the Holy Spirit. Holy Spirit, rise up within me as I praise God. I fully expect to speak with other tongues as You give me the utterance (Acts 2:4).

In Jesus' Name,

Amen!

About the Author

Pamela Christian Flickinger grew up in a small rural town as a preacher's daughter. Her Christian upbringing exposed her to religious extremes concerning such topics as judgment, law and grace, and freedom in the Spirit.

Her hunger to know God for herself drove her to experience the truth about God and His Word as a teenager. As she continued to grow in her relationship with her heavenly Father, she applied what she was learning after marrying and starting a family of her own.

After the birth of her second child, who was later diagnosed with eczema, her pursuits of God's Word grew stronger. It was during this time, *The Pocket Prayer* was birthed, and the victory won. Her revelation about the power in God's Word and how to apply it as a "pocket prayer" is simple, yet effective, no matter the circumstance.

May her revelation of God's faithfulness to His Word become your revelation as you read today!

For More Information

You can contact

Pamela Flickinger at:

pflick321@gmail.com

www.ingramcontent.com/pod-product-compliance
Lightning Source LLC
Chambersburg PA
CBHW072009110526
44592CB00012B/1249